He Lived on Our Street

Enduring Words for Today

by
Leslie R. Marston

Light and Life Press
Winona Lake, Indiana 46590

Printed in the United States of America
by Light and Life Press, Winona Lake, Indiana 46590

Copyright © 1979 by
Light and Life Press

ISBN 0-89367-042-1

TABLE OF CONTENTS

Introduction   5

1. He Lived on Our Street   7
2. Power for City Streets   17
3. When Jesus Comes to Our Town   29

RADIO

4. I Need a Chart   45
5. God's Answer to Man's Hunger   50

EDUCATION

6. Bring the Books   58
7. Rebels Against the Yoke   75

CHURCH AND SOCIETY

8. Evangelical Christianity in a Pagan Age   87
9. God and the Nations   109

CHURCH AND THEOLOGY

10. The River of Spiritual Life   122
11. The Continental Divide
    in Christian Doctrine   139
12. What It Means to Love God Perfectly   145
13. Faith Working by Love   157
14. The Mockery of Minimal Righteousness   177
15. The Church as the Body of Christ   190

ACTION

16. Redeeming the Time in Evil Days   210

INTRODUCTION

Bishop Leslie R. Marston served his church and the evangelical community for forty years before his retirement. Following that he led in the development of his denomination's historical and archival center.

Bishop Marston was a clear, forceful·exponent of evangelical Christianity. The messages presented here, you will agree, were prophetic. The timeless truths clear the bounds of dates and circumstances of their first utterance. Marston speaks with remarkable freshness and relevance to the issues we face as we approach the end of the twentieth century.

Marston's messages have style. It is ever clear, cogent, compact, and forceful. He deserves to be read by those seeking a model in written communication. His messages are needed now by teachers and ministers of the gospel. His logic is compelling. His interpretation of the Scriptures is direct and convincing. His sense of historical, social, and religious perspective illuminates his message. His stock-in-trade is the imperishable, not the fad.

Marston was our contemporary. His writings speak with eloquence to the issues in the present church, nation, world. His is a sane word in a paranoid world.

Publication of these messages is no exercise in

recognition, nostalgia, or giving honor. It is rather the re-utterance of timeless truth, aptly and presently applicable.

Lloyd H. Knox
Winona Lake, Indiana

Note: I have attempted to group Bishop Marston's messages in a few broad, helpful categories in the Table of Contents. Then in each instance there is brief notation as to content or circumstance regarding the message printed above each title.

LHK

*A sermon on the significance
of the Incarnation.*

He Lived on Our Street

"And the Word was made flesh

—and dwelt among us" (AV, ARV, RSV)
—and tabernacled among us" (J. Wesley)
—and tented among us" (Montgomery)
—and lived awhile in our midst" (Moffat)

By all these renderings of the original we must conclude that His was not a fleeting appearance — merely a glimpse — but an abiding presence; He actually lived with us, a man among men. Indeed we may say, *"He lived on our street!"*

Our text is not an incidental or offhand remark by John, the writer of this Gospel. He was making a point — a very important point, basic to the Christian faith. In fact, it is quite evident that a primary reason for John writing his Gospel was to combat wrong ideas concerning the Incarnation. The teaching that God in Christ actually became flesh and blood was disputed very early in Christian history — as early as apostolic days.

We tend to think of the Scripture as completely transcendent — "out of this world" and above the reach of our experience. Not so! Inspired as we believe the Scripture to be, it had a context in human history, in the living experience of men at a particular point in the past of the race. Yes, it belonged to its age — and the wonder of God's Word is its timelessness! Growing out of mankind's past, it nevertheless is eternal — true yesterday, today, and tomorrow. And so it speaks to our age, this closing period of the twentieth century, this Christmas season.

Now — what was the living context of our theme passage, "And the Word was made flesh and dwelt among us"? Simply this, that by the time John wrote his Gospel near the close of the first century, erroneous doctrines were gaining acceptance. This seriously threatened the apostolic church, by which is meant the Christian church during its period when the apostles — those who had been personal followers of our Lord, such as John himself — were still living and governing the church.

If we read our scripture lesson with proper emphasis, it changes from a rhythmic cadence of poetic beauty to become a staccato protest and contradiction of errors. These errors are three:

1. Jesus Christ's body was not physical in reality, but only appeared to be flesh. Matter is evil, and therefore, there could have been no incarnation — no union of God with flesh. *God in Christ could not have lived on our street.*

2. Or, if Christ's body indeed was flesh, like our bodies, then He could not actually have been divine but was merely an intermediate being residing in a human body — a being lesser than God although superior to man. Again, *God in Christ could not have lived on our street.*

3. Creation was not the handiwork of Christ, for God would not defile His hands with dirt! Jesus the Christ could not have been the Creator — or if Creator, then *not God* — but a lesser being intermediate between God and man. *God in Christ could not have lived on our street.*

Such were the views of the Gnostics, who, a little later, all but wrecked the Christian church by swinging it toward an inclusive paganism.

But there was another sect, closer in its origin to the Christian church, that had wrong ideas, denying the Incarnation. This was the Ebionite sect of Jewish Christians who would constrict Christianity to a legalistic humanism. They maintained that Jesus was a great man — but only a man. And therefore, of course, He had no preexistence and could have had no part in Creation. This sect finally took on Gnostic features, and it is probable that in our lesson John was contending against Gnosticism in its broad meaning. Therefore, in the following verses from chapter 1, note John's vigorous assertions against all who denied:

    1. Christ's essential humanity
    2. Christ's essential deity
    3. Christ as existing from eternity
    4. Christ as Creator, the maker of all things

We now reread the lesson from the first chapter of John — with his staccato emphasis:

    1. In the beginning *was* the Word, and the Word *was* with God, and the Word *was* God.
    2. The same *was* in the *beginning* with God.
    3. All things *were* made by him; and without him was not any thing made that was made.

4. In him *was* life; and the life was the *light* of men.

5. And the *light* shineth in darkness; and the darkness comprehended it not.

10. He *was* in the world, and the world *was* made by him, and the world knew him not.

14. And the Word *was* made flesh, and *dwelt* among *us,* (and we beheld his glory, the glory as of the only begotten of the Father,) full of grace and truth.

It was against similar errors that Paul had written:

> Beware lest any man spoil you through philosophy and vain deceit, after the tradition of men, after the rudiments of the world, and not after Christ. For in him dwelleth all the fulness of the Godhead bodily.
>
> Colossians 2:8-9

Paul here is saying that Christ was not some angel-like intermediary, neither God nor man. He is both God and man! He is not an emanation from God, falling away from Him to a lesser power and holiness — *but he is the fullness of deity manifest in the flesh!*

We are told that Christ's birth was not celebrated in the early centuries of the Church, probably because the apostles and Early Church fathers were more concerned with the completed work of Christ on the Cross, and with His following resurrection and ascension. But in time, the Church began the celebration of Christ's birth in order (some think) to combat the heresies of the day — that Christ was not God incarnate, that Christ's birth, His body, His

10

sufferings were not real but only appearances, only a stage play!

These errors, against which John and Paul contended, were but the beginnings of a long series of heresies under different names; but below the surface they were essentially the same false doctrines opposed by the apostles. Such robbing Christ of His essential deity continues to this day.

And yet, after all the centuries of vain philosophizing concerning God's relationship to Jesus Christ in the Incarnation, the Christian doctrine that Jesus was indeed the Incarnation of God holds in our day.

> Veiled in flesh the Godhead see;
>   Hail th'incarnate Deity!
> Pleased as man with men to dwell,
>   Jesus, our Emmanuel.
>
> Charles Wesley

Indeed this is a mystery, how the human and the Divine could be perfectly united in Jesus Christ so that He was "as divine as the Father, yet as human as ourselves." But if we are truly Christian in our faith, we accept this "mystery of godliness." Its statement comes to us down through the centuries as the second of our "Articles of Religion," a truth etched clearly in the creed of the Church by crucial conflict with error. Here it is:

> The Son, who is the Word of the Father, the very and eternal God, of one substance with the Father, took man's nature in the womb of the blessed virgin, so that the two whole and perfect natures, that is to say, the Godhood and manhood, were joined together in one

person, never to be divided, whereof is one Christ, very God and very man, who truly suffered, was crucified, dead and buried, to be the one mediator between God and man, by the sacrifice of Himself both for original sin and for the actual transgressions of men.

Free Methodist *Book of Discipline,* 1964, par. 22

* * *

If Jesus indeed was human, He must pass through stages of development as is nature's course. As He himself said of nature's order, "First the blade, then the ear, after that the full corn in the ear" (Mark 4:28).

Yes, "He lived on our street"; first a babe in Bethlehem's manger, with the limitations of infancy apart from sin; "He lived on our street," a child in Nazareth . . . as a lad running over Galilean hills . . . as a youth in His father's carpenter shop. . . as a young man in the prime of early maturity, by profession a rabbi or teacher, leading a group of patience-testing pupils . . . in Galilee, Judea, Perea, Samaria.

It is interesting that of the four Gospel writers, Luke the physician said of Jesus: "And Jesus increased in wisdom and stature, and in favor with God and man" (Luke 2:52). It was a fourfold development: *intellectual, physical, spiritual, social.* If Jesus was fully human, He must have been tempted as we are tempted. The Scriptures validate this.

For verily he took not on him the nature of angels; but he took on him the seed of Abraham. Wherefore in all things it behooved him to be made like unto his brethren, that he might be a merciful and faithful high

12

priest in things pertaining to God, to make reconciliation for the sins of the people. For in that he himself hath suffered being tempted, he is able to succor them that are tempted.   Hebrews 2:16-18

For we have not a high priest which cannot be touched with the feeling of our infirmities; but was in all points tempted like as we are, yet without sin.
                                                Hebrews 4:15-16

The temptations that came to Jesus, even in His maturity, have puzzled many. W. Robertson Nicoll, in his book on the life of Jesus, said what should be helpful to us all: "We do not attempt to explain how the sinless Christ could be tempted. We assume that a sinless manhood can be tempted. . . ."

This is it: He was tempted in His humanity — and in all points as we are tempted — and met temptation as you and I must meet it. He laid hold of resources that are yours and mine; and He overcame, not as the Son of God of infinite power, but as the Son of Man of perfect purity and unwavering faith.

Note the temptation to turn stones into bread. After forty days of testing in the wilderness, "If thou be the Son of God, command that these stones be made bread" (Matthew 4:3). Note His answer: "It is written, Man shall not live by bread alone, but by every word that proceedeth out of the mouth of God" (v. 4).

We have the same sword of defense that He wielded, the Word of God. But we must note something more: He refused to meet Satan on the issue of His divinity. Satan had with great subtlety suggested to Jesus a doubt concerning His relationship to His Heavenly Father: "*If* thou be the son of

God, . . ." This taunt of Satan, in effect a dare: "Prove it, now, *if* you are the Son of God. Turn stones into bread to save yourself from starving here in the wilderness. I dare you!"

With calm composure Jesus answered, "It is written, *Man*. . . ." In effect He is saying, "I'm here as the Son of *man,* and I will meet this ordeal as the sons of men must meet temptation. I will not thwart or withdraw the Incarnation by stooping to meet your dare."

Thank God! Jesus did not forsake His humanity, and ours, in the time of temptation. And so we have this assurance that "He lived on our street!"

Again, of Christ's full humanity we have, in John 4:6 the account of the midday stop of Jesus and some of His disciples for rest and food and drink at Jacob's well on their journey through Samaria. Judging by the distance from Jerusalem, it must have been near noon of the second day of the journey that they reached this point. "Jesus. . . , being wearied with his journey, sat thus on the well: and it was about the sixth hour," i.e., high noon.

Here was the Word made flesh — weary on the journey of life.

> Though he were a Son, yet learned he obedience by the things which he suffered; and being made perfect, he became the author of eternal salvation unto all them that obey him.   Hebrews 5:8-9

> For it became him, for whom are all things, and by whom are all things, in bringing many sons unto glory, to make the captain of their salvation perfect through sufferings.   Hebrews 2:10

You see, Jesus was obedient unto law — the very laws that bind you and me — for "He lived on our street," as one of us! He was obedient unto the laws of:

1. Physiology — fatigue, hunger, thirst.
2. Physics — gravity.
3. Biology — growth and development.
4. Psychology — trial, temptation, emotional reaction.
5. Sociology — dependence upon others: He must remain hungry until the disciples return with food; thirsty until someone with neighborly spirit draws water for Him.

Jesus went the full distance of our humanity — even unto death. Yes, He lived — and suffered — and died "on our street"!

* * *

Why did God come to earth as the Son of Man? That we sons of men — you and I — might become the sons of God (see John 3:16). Someone has stated very simply the purpose of the Incarnation:

Christ came to bring God near;
Christ came to make God clear;
Christ came to make God dear.

And it is difficult to say more than these words convey:

Jesus lived on our street, and brought God near;
By living on our street, Jesus made God clear;
By living on our street, He showed us that God is love, and made Him dear — an indwelling heart-reality.

I like the lines of Henry More who, back in the seventeenth century, wrote:

The Son of God thus man became,
  That men the Sons of God might be,
And by their second birth regain
  A likeness to His deity.

Because Jesus came as the babe in Bethlehem's manger, because He grew as a child in stature and in wisdom and in favor with God and man, because as a man He was wearied by life's journey and must rest and refresh His spent body, because He was in all points tempted like as we are — yet without sin — we know we have a high priest touched by our infirmities and we may, "Therefore come boldly to the throne of grace, that we may obtain mercy, and find grace to help in time of need" (Hebrews 4:16).

This babe in a manger, this lad in the Temple, this Teacher who spake as never man spake, was not God wearing loosely a robe of flesh as a human mask, acting a human part on the world stage as merely an example toward which man must ever strive while ever doomed to fail. But in Him, God took upon himself not alone the form but also the very nature of man. As someone has expressed it, He was no naturalized foreigner here on earth, but He was born here!

And *He lived on our street!*

Gifts and preparation
for service are important.
The Holy Spirit is the Giver
of the indispensable power for the Church's
life-changing mission.

Power for City Streets

But ye shall receive power, after that the Holy Ghost
is come upon you: and ye shall be witnesses unto me
both in Jerusalem, and in all Judea, and in Samaria,
and unto the uttermost part of the earth.   Acts 1:8

More than nineteen centuries ago, Jesus told a
small band of men who had loved Him and had
thought that He was to be a king that they were to
establish His kingdom after He had departed — by
carrying His message to the ends of the earth.

But not one of them felt equal to the task to
which He had commissioned them. Earlier, they had
eagerly asked Him when He was going to do it —
Now? "Wilt thou at this time restore again the
kingdom to Israel?" They thought the task was *His*
— but He had answered, "Ye shall be witnesses unto
me . . . unto the uttermost part of the earth."

As the Lord's commission and command fell from
His lips, one by one the disciples' heads fell and
their countenances reflected their inner fear and
confusion. They were embarrassed. I can believe they
reacted in various ways as Jesus spoke:

—"Ye shall be witnesses unto me . . . in
Jerusalem." At this point Peter's head dropped, and

he edged back behind his fellows, desiring to be lost in the crowd. He had so miserably failed in witnessing in Jerusalem not long before. He had denied his Lord repeatedly, and he knew he was not ready to witness to his Lord in Jerusalem.

—"Ye shall be witnesses unto me in Samaria." I can well believe that the brothers, James and John, looked at each other abashed because they remembered the time when in Samaria they had asked Jesus to call down fire on Samaritans who would not accept them or receive them in their village. The Lord rebuked them on that occasion. They didn't want to go back to Samaria and witness to Christ. They weren't ready to witness in Samaria!

—"Ye shall be witnesses unto me unto the uttermost part of the earth." Thomas was distressed — Thomas who had said he would not believe the witness of his brethren until he had seen, until he had touched the nail prints. And here Jesus is telling them to go to the ends of the earth and witness to those who had never seen and never would see in this life the resurrected Lord. And Thomas wasn't ready.

And not one of the Eleven volunteered. Not one stood forward and said, "Here am I, send me!" But Isaiah didn't say that, either, until something happened to him. That something hadn't yet happened to these disciples. They didn't volunteer because they weren't ready.

But what was their lack?

Was it money? They were poor men, every one of them. Their treasurer had been pilfering their funds. Yes, they did lack money. Did Jesus then say to them, "Tarry in the city of Jerusalem until you have put on a financial campaign and have a substantial bank account, and then, backed with cash, you can pay your passage to the ends of the earth with a witness"?

Did He say to the disciples, "Tarry in Jerusalem to contact some of the wealthy men who have been favorable to our cause. There is Joseph of Arimathea who contributed his new tomb for my burial, but I vacated the tomb — he has it again. Perhaps he would give the cold cash equivalent of that tomb which I have relinquished"?

Did He tell them that Nicodemus had followed and believed — but secretly — for fear of his fellows of the Jewish church? . . . that perhaps if Nicodemus were approached, he would satisfy his uneasy conscience by supporting them — anonymously, of course, but still giving generously — for he was a rich man?

No, our Lord didn't say anything about money. Money was not the first essential. Money was not the thing that was needed most.

Although not of the first importance, money is important. It is power, and for that reason it is dangerous when it is placed first in our lives or in any cause which we represent. Roger Babson, the great economist, has said, "Money seems so powerful that it makes men forget the supreme power."

Money is important in the building of His church here on earth. The cattle on a thousand hills, and the gold in those hills, are His; but in the building of His church here on earth, He has no cattle but yours and mine — no gold but the gold you and I hold in stewardship, for we are workers together with Him. It has also been said, "God builds no churches! By His plan, that labor has been left to man. The humblest church demands its price in human toil and sacrifice."

But if money was not what the disciples principally lacked, was then their crucial lack that of learning and eloquence, talent, and culture? They lacked all of these, for they were simple, untutored, uneducated men. They weren't stupid, by any means; but they hadn't been trained in the University of Jerusalem at the feet of Gamaliel as was Saul of Tarsus who became Paul, the great Apostle and missionary to the Gentile world.

Although they lacked talent, culture, and education, our Lord did not say, "Well, you'd better wait until you've met the entrance requirements of the University of Jerusalem and have enrolled under Dr. Gamaliel. And while you're there, be sure to keep your eyes open and locate the promising students who would add prestige and importance to our movement. There's a young man there named Saul of Tarsus with a great future before him in some direction or cause. Enlist him!"

That isn't the way our Lord talked to them. Although they were without learning and culture, our Lord didn't indicate they could not be witnesses until they had completed their education.

Education, talent, and culture are important, if they are subordinated to the task of making Christ known to the world. Our Lord has laid His hand on men of training, qualifications, culture, and talent down through the crises of history. There were

Moses, Daniel, Isaiah, Paul, Luther, Wesley, and our Free Methodist founder, Roberts. These are only a few of those of unusual qualifications, not only by nature, but also by culture and training. But with learning and culture only, man's efforts are futile.

John Wesley was a man of great natural powers and of acquired culture. He was well equipped but impotent until he had that something more. He said of himself concerning his early preaching on his father's circuit, "I drew no crowds, I alarmed no consciences, I preached much but saw no fruit of my labors." But later came his heartwarming and his soul-stirring. After that, he had great revivals. Multitudes hung upon his words, and many were brought into the kingdom of grace. Concerning his success, he didn't say, "I gave them literature. I gave them history. I gave them metaphysics, logic, science." He was in command of the knowledge of his day along all these lines. But this man of learning, a teacher of logic in Oxford University, would say after he had preached the Word of God, "I gave them Christ."

If neither money nor culture was the disciples' primary lack when the Lord gave the Great Commission and then left them, was prestige their lack? Was it recognition by earthly powers or ecclesiastical organization?

Did our Lord say to them, "You are men of no reputation: you have no influence in society. You'd better wait until you have enlisted a few who have influence, and then send them to the councils and the Sanhedrin. Perhaps you could then even send a delegation to Rome to lobby the senate and get the

Caesar on your side. When you have the power of the mighty Roman empire back of you, you can go anywhere with my message''?

No, our Lord didn't say that. He was talking to ordinary men with nicknames such as Jack and Jim, Pete and Andy, and Matt and Nat and Phil. He still didn't tell them that prestige was their essential need. He had told them that they would be delivered to the councils; that they would be brought before the synagogues and beaten by their fellow Jews; that they would be brought before rulers and kings for His sake. He did not tell them that they were to win their way by prestige and influence.

Jesus said not one word about their need of money, learning, or worldly standing. Yes, they needed these, if they would rightly use them, but these are incidental. One thing is imperative! What is it?

We read that the officials who brought Peter and John to trial because of the tumult that followed the healing of the lame man ''perceived that they were unlearned and ignorant men, [and] they marveled; and they took knowledge of them, that they had been with Jesus'' (Acts 4:13), and had learned of Him.

And that is the authority that the Christian must have!

When these rulers ordered Peter and John ''not to speak at all nor teach in the name of Jesus,'' they replied, ''We cannot but speak the things which we have seen and heard.'' The very task of a witness! Charles Wesley has put that declaration in the form of verse in one of his hymns:

What we have felt and seen
With confidence we tell,
And publish to the souls of men
The signs infallible.

How Peter and John now differ from their cowardice a few weeks earlier when both forsook Him and Peter so emphatically denied Him! Then they had lacked the power of the Holy Spirit. Now they had tarried until they received the very power by which Jesus himself had wrought and taught! Witnessing does not depend upon the wealth we have, upon the talent and knowledge we possess, nor upon prestige. With limited amounts of these very desirable things, we can witness if we have the power of the Holy Spirit within.

So now we have the answer: What the disciples lacked, and what kept them from stepping forward as volunteers to go to the end of the earth with a witness, was the very power by which the Christ himself had witnessed while here on earth. We read that at His baptism the Spirit descended as a dove upon Him. After His baptism, He was led of the Spirit into the wilderness to be tempted of Satan; and after the temptation, He returned in the power of the Spirit into Galilee. The record states that in Nazareth "when he had opened the book, he found the place where it is written, The Spirit of the Lord is upon me," and He made direct application of that passage from the prophet to His own life and ministry and mission.

Very clearly, He is saying to the disciples that they are to receive the power of the very Spirit by which He ministered. The Church is to be the

continuing body of Jesus Christ here on earth, and
His Spirit will possess that body and empower it to
carry the gospel to the end of the earth. Listen to the
words of the poetess:

> Christ has no hands but our hands
> To do His work today;
> He has no feet but our feet
> To lead men in His way;
> He has no tongue but our tongues
> To tell men how He died;
> He has no help but our help
> To bring them to His side.
>
> Annie Johnson Flint

The early Church started well on its world-
changing mission. After it received the power of the
Holy Spirit, it rapidly extended its witness throughout the Roman Empire. But with the official
acceptance of Christianity by the Empire under
Constantine, dark days came. The Church, prosper-
ing in poverty and persecution, faltered in prosperity. It lagged on its mission. Money, culture, political
power clogged this body of Christ and hampered its
movement, even as heavy weights.

There have come times when the genius of early
Christianity has been rediscovered and the quickening Spirit has broken through all hindrances to bring
revival — only to subside again into priestly
uniformity, replacing "prophetic fire" with "painted
fire," as John Wesley called it.

And now, after nearly twenty centuries of
Christianity, the world rests on the crumbling edge
of a volcano — a volcano ready at any moment to
erupt and destroy our very civilization!

How has this come about? The Church has not carried out its mission; it has loitered on its way to the ends of the earth with the gospel message, by which message the hearts of men were to be changed; it has loitered until the minds of men have advanced to the conquest of nature's forces with hearts still evil!

In the last century, Herbert Spencer declared that to educate reason without changing desire is to place high-powered guns in the hands of savages. Spencer's figure of speech is still effective, but he knew not the infinitely greater destructive powers to be developed in this century.

Today, men of shrewd and trained minds and skilled hands, but of wicked hearts and evil desires, are playing with forces that can destroy the world as we know it. Hence, "men's hearts [are] failing them for fear." Command of power without self-command and holy desires spells tragedy for the world itself.

This age is not a thoughtful age, is not a contemplative age. It is an active age, a dynamic age. Power is what men are seeking, and science is bringing power within the command of men's minds and hands to an amazing degree. But while in terms of natural power, we are now in the atomic age and the space age, in the religious world we are little beyond horse-and-buggy power. Oh, the tragedy of it!

Is our Lord's promise of spiritual power for world conquest outdated? Has atomic power eclipsed the power of the Holy Ghost and made it ineffective? Is the gospel in our day no longer the power of God unto salvation as it was in Paul's day in the mighty Roman Empire?

Nothing can save our world today but the power of God changing men's hearts. Social betterment, education, and all the schemes of men to bring Utopia work too slowly to avert the impending destruction — nor could they alone save the world, even with unlimited time!

But to save the world, the power of God must be channeled through human personality — moving human hands and feet and tongues, stirring human hearts, illuminating human minds, surcharging every capacity of redeemed human personality. This power of God does not operate in a vacuum, insulated from the world of sinners that must be saved.

But too many Christians today are like the disciples when Jesus told them they were to take His message to the whole world. They are not ready. They lack the Spirit's power. Timorous and fearful, they live behind closed doors, shut away in upper rooms.

The disciples were to *tarry* — not abide in seclusion. To *tarry* means "to be momentarily on the point of departure." It does not mean to settle down in a permanent residence.

And Jesus did not send them to the wilderness to await the Spirit's coming. Tarrying in the wilderness might lead them to build tabernacles and there abide, shut away from the world's need and unconscious of their own lack of power!

But they were to tarry in the *city*. There they would be aware of the city's need, its sin, its suffering; but also, by its need, made keenly aware of their own lack of power to meet the needs of city streets — of human society.

The urge to the wilderness sometimes is strong. Sensing our own weakness, we shrink from being a channel of power lest we lose the little power we have. We would rather be a reservoir than a channel. So we build a dam to hoard our religion. We prefer the quiet of seclusion, the shelter of the sanctuary, the safety of the wilderness.

Such was the psalmist's longing: "Oh that I had wings like a dove! For then would I fly away, and be at rest. Lo, then would I wander far off, and remain in the wilderness. . . . I would hasten my escape from the windy storm and tempest . . . for I have seen violence and strife in the city" (Psalm 55:6-9).

But the power of the Holy Spirit, outpoured on the Day of Pentecost, sent the disciples from their closed-door, upper-room seclusion into the streets where men and women jostled and strove in need and in sin.

Such is the purpose of Pentecost: to fit Christians for city streets — so that they no longer need isolate themselves to protect their piety.

And Christ is there — in the streets! Even as He promised, "Lo, I am with you alway, even unto the end of the world."

What Christ Said

I said: "Let me walk in the fields."
　　He said: "No, walk in the town."
I said: "There are no flowers there."
　　He said: "No flowers, but a crown."

I said: "But the skies are black;
　　There is nothing but noise and din."

And He wept as He sent me back;
  "There is more," He said, "there is sin."

I said: "But the air is thick,
  And fogs are veiling the sun."
He answered: "Yet souls are sick,
  And souls in the dark, undone."

I said: "I shall miss the light,
  And friends will miss me, they say."
He answered: "Choose tonight
  If *I* am to miss you, or they."

I pleaded for time to be given.
  He said: "Is it hard to decide?
It will not seem hard in heaven
  To have followed the steps of your Guide."

I cast one look at the fields,
  Then set my face to the town.
He said: "My child, do you yield?
  Will you leave the flowers for the crown?"

Then into His hand went mine;
  And into my heart came He;
And I walk in a light divine,
  The path I had feared to see.

George Macdonald

*First published in 1961
in a collection of sermons
compiled and edited
by Andrew W. Blackwood*

WHEN JESUS COMES TO OUR TOWN

When he was come into Jerusalem, all the city was
moved, saying, who is this?　　　　　　Matthew 21:10
　　　　　　　　　　　　　　　　　　　Read 21:1-17

Our text refers to that first Palm Sunday, when
the Lord Jesus entered Jerusalem as King. In
addition to the many thousands who lived there, the
city was crowded with multitudes of pilgrims who
had come to celebrate the approaching Passover.
Whether they accepted or rejected Him, those motley
throngs could not mistake this Peasant's claim to
Kingship. He had ridden into the city on an
unbroken colt and had composedly accepted palm-
waving and hosannas from a joyous retinue of fellow
peasants.

Until now He has restrained His enthusiastic
followers when they would take Him and make Him
their King. Hitherto, His time had not come. But
now the time is at hand for Him to confront the
world with His claims to supreme allegiance. Well
does He know that those who reject Him as King
will seek to destroy Him on a Roman cross, as
though He were a knave. In much the same spirit

our Lord comes into our town today. How then does He come?

HE COMES AS PRINCE OF PEACE

Our Lord did not force His claim to Kingship by riding to conquest on a panoplied charger and at the head of a revolutionary army. Long since, He had met and overcome the temptation to resort to the power of marching hosts as the means of bringing deliverance to a captive people and of ushering in the acceptable year of the Lord. From an exceeding high mountain Satan had given Him a glimpse of the kingdoms of the world and all their glory, not only in that age but also in every age to come. Satan had suggested that by bowing down at the shrine of organized political power Jesus could at once bring to pass the millennium of righteousness.

At once our Lord discerned the evil source of the suggestion. Promptly He ordered the devil to depart: "Get thee hence, Satan: for it is written, Thou shalt worship the Lord thy God, and him only shalt thou serve" (Matthew 4:10). The tempter had appealed to Jesus to worship the power of the State, but our Lord saw clearly that a man must bow down in subjection to the object of His worship, and so it has been down through all the intervening ages. Would-be saviours of the world, who worship military and political power, have become the slaves of that power. Instead of delivering the world, they have become its scourges.

Today the Lord Jesus would make clear the peaceful means by which He would establish His kingdom, and also the peaceful character of that

30

kingdom. On the first Palm Sunday He sought these ends by the simple pageantry of His entry into Jerusalem on a colt that had never submitted to human command, and therefore according to tradition was suited to sacred service. Furthermore, His retinue was not a regiment of soldiers with plumed helmets and shining shields, but a band of simple, devoted followers, on this occasion augmented by a throng of pilgrims from other provinces and foreign lands, all of them on their way to the feast. And lest any should question His intentions, notwithstanding these clear evidences that He had come in peace, He would shortly declare before Pontius Pilate: "My kingdom is not of this world: if my kingdom were of this world, then would my servants fight" (John 18:36a). Today our Lord is still the Prince of Peace.

HE CANNOT ENLIST THE FICKLE

"When he was come into Jerusalem, all the city was moved, saying, Who is this?" To this question the invading multitude had a ready answer. Before Jesus they had spread their garments as a ready carpet. From olive and palm trees they had stripped branches to wave in His honor. To Him as the Son of David they had cried aloud their hosannas. Throughout the surrounding region the exciting news about the recent raising of Lazarus had spread near and far and had greeted hosts of pilgrims as they came up to Jerusalem. Many of these pilgrims, as well as others native to the area, were ready to believe in Jesus as the Deliverer of Israel; and now the drama of the procession had caught them up in its mood and its movement. At the moment it seemed easy to believe that Jesus of Nazareth was indeed the Son of David, the long-promised Messiah. Therefore, to the query of curious, skeptical, and scornful residents of Jerusalem, "Who is this?" there burst from the lips of joyous marchers the spontaneous response: "This is Jesus, the prophet of Nazareth!"

By His acceptance of their plaudits, our Lord acknowledged the acclaim of the shouting throng. But since He knew what was in man, even then He could hear the distant roar of the raging mob, which within a few short days would include some of these very same persons, their ringing hosannas now changed into raucous demands: "Away with him! Crucify him!" Yes, even in the multitude that marched with Jesus on His day of triumph there were fickle followers. There may have been some whose belief in Him as the Messiah was based primarily on such signs and wonders as the raising of Lazarus, but who knew nothing of an intimate personal fellowship with Jesus as their abiding Redeemer.

In His parable about the four kinds of soil, He had already pictured such unstable folk. The fickle are those who joyfully receive the truth into stony, shallow soil, where it quickly sprouts and for a time seems to flourish. But with no deep roots the grain soon withers away under the scorching heat of tribulation and persecution. In our own day, when the Lord comes to our town to work spiritual and moral reform He may for a while gather a throng enthusiastic for the cause of the righteousness that He proclaims. But when opposition develops, when economic and other pressures are applied by malignant groups that seek to turn the tide against the truth, the fickle ones desert what has become an unpopular cause. Some of them even scream with the crowd, ''Release unto us Barabbas!''

HE OPPOSES THE SECULARISTS

Christ's entrance into Jerusalem as Ruler challenged the rule of King Midas within the Temple. Mark says that Jesus entered into the Temple ''and looked round about on all things.'' In the Court of the Gentiles He saw secularists who sold beasts and fowls for use as sacrifices, and others who for a price exchanged foreign money into Temple coins. Soon they learned that Christ as Lord would not tolerate their god of gain. To accept His reign in their lives would mean to renounce their secularism and their sacrilege, and this they would never do.

Those secularists must have recalled the sudden appearance of this prophet from Nazareth on an earlier occasion. Then His burning indignation lashed out against the traders, and He drove their beasts out of the Temple. Now they feel enraged because His flaming gaze has found them again at their profane business. So they are not surprised when the Reformer, recently proclaimed their King, again ''went into the temple of God, and cast out all them that sold and bought in the temple, and overthrew the tables of the money changers, and the seats of them that sold doves, and said unto them, It is written, My house shall be called the house of prayer; but ye have made it a den of thieves'' (Matthew 21:12-13).

Today when Jesus comes to our town, again He looks "round about on all things." Even in the Temple He beholds things that He cannot approve. He discerns that some make merchandise of church membership, joining the popular or moneyed congregation of the town for business and social advantage. He may find that the house of prayer has become a place for carnal feasting and carnival pleasures, thus competing with the amusement world so as to gain a few shekels to support the church and attract adherents. Jesus finds also that some who confess His name are corrupt in their business practices. Others oppress the fatherless and the widow by a legal advantage that wealth and power often make possible, or else they deny laborers their just wages.

Christ challenges all such secularism. He declares that everyone must choose between His Lordship and that of money. "Christ will be Lord of all, or He will not be Lord at all." No one can serve two masters. There can be no "percentage Christians," half for Him and half against Him. Those who choose to serve Him are changed by His grace. Then their changed lives work changes in the community. Such is the leaven of righteousness. When Jesus comes into our town, everything becomes transformed in the life of the one who receives Him as King.

HE REBUKES THE SELF-RIGHTEOUS

After Jesus cleansed the House of God from profit-seeking secularists, "the blind and the lame came to him, in the temple; and he healed them." Also, "he taught daily in the temple." Thus He restored the Temple to its proper uses: worship, teaching, and healing. By so doing He enraged the leaders of the Church, the chief priests and the scribes, the Pharisees and the elders of the people, so that those leaders "sought to destroy him." Those men should have been the last to resent the cleansing of the Temple and its restoration as God's house of prayer. But their authority had been openly ignored and defied. In Jewish society those men constituted an order of tremendous power, a power, humanly speaking, sufficient to bring the Son of God to death on the Cross. That was to be their revenge.

Under their leadership the religious and moral life of the people had been reduced to barren formulas that stunted or prevented the growth of men's souls. At every turn those so-called "religious" leaders met life with a prescription. They had all the answers, which left no room for faith in God. Upon the bowed shoulders of weary men those leaders piled heavy burdens, which they themselves would not touch with a little finger. They gave far more heed to traditions than to the Scriptures. They felt more concern about a footnote than about a Bible text. They deciphered marginal notations and multiplied commentaries, while they ignored Christ's commandment of love. Such emphasis on non-essentials led to neglect of the things that matter most, and thus gave us the word "Pharisaism."

Our Lord's teaching about love and grace ill fitted such a legalistic and moralistic temper. How persistently He attempted to puncture the conceit of those scribes and those Pharisees! How strenuously He strove to break through their complacency and their self-satisfaction! With what vigor He pushed

His attacks on their neatly rationalized defenses! The strongest language He ever used in denouncing evil He directed against their self-righteousness. Once He spoke to them: "Ye hypocrites, well did Isaiah prophesy of you, saying, This people draweth nigh unto me with their mouth, and honoreth me with their lips; but their heart is far from me. But in vain they do worship me, teaching for doctrines the commandments of men" (Matthew 15:7-9). What bitter, biting, barbed words! And during that eventful week after the cleansing of the Temple, the Lord Jesus was to pronounce on those scribes and Pharisees a series of woes, climaxing them all with the severest condemnation: "Ye serpents, ye generation of vipers, how can ye escape the damnation of hell" (Matthew 23:33)?

When Jesus comes to our town today the authorities still become agitated, and sometimes they feel enraged. Both in church and in civic councils, rulers feel alarmed when their abuse of power to enslave men is challenged by the truth of God that sets men free. Power is perilous, far more so than the money that often provides the means to corrupt the use of power. Among the mighty not many surrender to the claims of God's truth, but when persons in authority do make that surrender their sophistication drops away. No longer do they feel that they have all the answers. Meekly one of them asks, with that newly converted Pharisee, Saul of Tarsus, "Lord, what wilt thou have me to do?" Once in a while a self-righteous "religious" ruler courageously faces the challenge of God's truth, and yields his enslaving grip on church or community to the redeeming power of Christ's love. A town with cleansed temples of worship and justice is a far better place for all who dwell therein, especially for. God's blessed little boys and girls.

He Instructs His Disciples

Once again look at the jubilant procession of those who stirred Jerusalem by their acclamation of Christ as King. Among them see His devoted disciples, especially the Twelve, who have daily lived in His company. By communion with Him, and by witnessing repeated manifestations of His power, they have been fully convinced of His Messiahship. In spreading palms before Him as King, and in hailing Him with loud hosannas, the Twelve have led the way. They are not among His fair-weather friends, who within a few days will shift their allegiance to Barabbas and cry out for the crucifixion of Christ.

But the days just ahead were to try the souls of the disciples and to discover even in them a streak of cowardice. That cowardice arose out of their perplexity and dismay when He whom they had acclaimed as King permitted Himself to be betrayed, convicted as a criminal, and then sentenced to death, with never a lightning stroke for defense and deliverance. In the triumphal march on Palm Sunday they had felt certain that He was the Messiah and that He would at once establish His kingdom. But even while marching in that procession there were many things that they could not understand. Indeed, the very events that marked the fulfillment of prophecy had escaped them. As John

37

reported later, ''These things understood not his disciples at the first: but when Jesus was glorified, then remembered they that these things were written of him, and that they had done these things unto him'' (John 12:16).

What was the root misunderstanding from which sprang so many of the disciples' perplexities and mistakes? Surely it was their fixed idea that Jesus was at that time to restore to Israel a temporal kingdom, with Him on an earthly throne, and with the Twelve as a Cabinet of His chief advisers. In all their words and their deeds this mistaken idea had repeatedly come to the surface. After the Transfiguration, while on the way to Capernaum, the Twelve had reasoned among themselves about which of them should be first in the kingdom. On that journey, before their argument had developed, He had explained to them that He must travel all the way to the Cross.

But the disciples were so obsessed with thoughts about the King who would parcel out to each of them a measure of His authority that they could give little heed to the Cross. They were too busy debating about which of them would be first in authority, Prime Minister in His Cabinet. What a spiritual distance lay between the Master, whose path already lay under the deepening shadow of the Cross, and His disciples, with their bickerings about rank and preferment in the kingdom that they did not begin to comprehend!

Afterward, while on His way up to Jerusalem for the last time, only a few days before the Triumphal Entry, our Lord had told the disciples all that awaited Him soon. But "they understood none of these things: ... neither knew they the things that were spoken" (Luke 18:34). And then, almost immediately after this solemn warning, James and John, with their ambitious mother, had sought out Jesus to ask that in His Kingdom one of them might sit on the right hand and one on His left. When the other disciples had discovered this conniving for the chief portfolios in the Cabinet, they had felt enraged. Alas, some of them had cherished lofty ambitions. But the Lord had rebuked them with the declaration that he who would be first among men must qualify by being servant of them all.

And so when Jesus comes to our town today, or any day, His followers have much to learn about the nature of the kingdom, the tests of discipleship, and the meaning of the Cross. At times with puzzled discouragement we may have said, with the two disciples on the road to Emmaus: "We trusted that it had been he which should have redeemed Israel" (Luke 24:21a). But when He has patiently made clear to us "in all the scriptures the things concerning himself," and has revealed himself in the humble sacrament of daily living, we know anew that He is our King. Once again our hearts burn with passionate loyalty to His claims on our total allegiance.

HE BLESSES THE CHILDREN

In the triumphal procession on that first Palm Sunday children took a leading part. Little boys and girls always take delight in a parade. On this occasion they were eagerly running before and after, vigorously waving their branches from palm trees, and with their sweet treble voices swelling the chorus of hosannas. Surely their devotion brought a smile to the face of the One who always had loved children. Nor did their devotion lag when the procession ended. On the morrow, after He had cleansed the Temple, and while He was teaching, the singing of the children, "Hosanna to the son of David," sorely displeased the chief priests and the scribes, so that they complained to our Lord: "Hearest thou what these say?" Then He answered: "Yea; have ye never read, Out of the mouth of babes and sucklings thou hast perfected praise" (Matthew 21:16)?

The Lord Jesus always had time for children. Not long before this experience in the Temple, the disciples had rebuked parents who desired Him to lay His hands on their children and bless them. But Jesus "was much displeased, and said unto them, Suffer the little children to come unto me, and forbid them not, for of such is the at earlier occasion when the disciples had been angrily debating about the merits of candidates for the premiership of the kingdom, Jesus had called a little child and placed him in their midst. Ordinarily that would be an embarrassing experience for a tiny tot among a dozen grown men, nearly all of them strangers. But no child ever ran away from the Master. Trustingly and at once this little fellow toddled into His outstretched arms. Then our Lord told the disciples: "Verily I say unto you, Except ye be converted, and become as little children, ye shall not enter into the kingdom of heaven. Whosoever therefore shall humble himself as this little child, the same is greatest in the kingdom of heaven" (Matthew 18:3-4).

What a contrast! How often in His earthly ministry must Jesus have turned away from adult complacency about kingdom matters, such as He found even among the disciples, and from the haughty legalism of the scribes and Pharisees, to the naturalness, the genuineness, the absorbing interests of a little child. When all around He saw closed minds, hardened hearts, and settled destinies, He could find refreshment in one of these little ones, dear to the heart of His Heavenly Father.

On this Palm Sunday the same Lord Jesus has come to our town. Here He would teach us that we are to have the zest and the alertness, the simple faith and the courageous spirit of childhood. When we lose our enthusiasms and can see nothing of wonder in a sunset, in the personality of a saint, or in the written Word of God, we have lost the spirit of childhood. And when our minds are closed to truth, so that we think we have the answers to all the world's questions, we have grown old without God.

HE BRINGS US LIGHT

As the Light of the world, the Lord Jesus fulfills the implied promise of old: "Unto the upright there ariseth light in the darkness" (Psalm 112:4a). He has done so in a small village of Central India. On a Saturday evening we journeyed to Umri, so isolated that once we had to travel along a river bed, where the deep sand trapped and stalled our automobile. But at journey's end we found that Jesus had gone before us into the village. That night we looked into the faces of a throng of villagers. Some of them sat on rugs, and others standing fringed the assembly that had gathered under a large awning stretched across the main street for this occasion.

With the chief of the village as one of their leaders, those dusky, bright-eyed villagers praised God with instruments and songs that sounded strange and even weird to our Western ears. But God heard those instruments, understood those songs, and accepted those offerings of praise. In that village the coming of the Lord Jesus has wrought a marvelous change, for light had arisen in their darkness. So we rejoiced that night as we picked our way "home" through the darkness, sometimes missing the trail, and again sinking into the sand of the river bed. Hence it was midnight when we reached the hospital compound and at last settled down for brief but restful sleep.

Morning soon came with a glorious light. It was Palm Sunday, and I may never again on earth witness such a beautiful scene. In a triumphal march round the spacious compound a throng of villagers from nearby Umri, with residents of the hospital compound — men and women, boys and girls, clad in colorful oriental garb — came singing about Jesus and waving palm branches. Most moving of all was the conclusion of the exercises. Before the residence where we were guests a band of small children rendered an exercise consisting of songs, with the waving of palms.

In the heart of that non-Christian land our souls were refreshed beyond measure by this beautiful observance of a great Christian festival. That morning the compassionate Father in heaven looked down with delight upon those children of far-off India, ever dear to His heart. Like the boys and girls on the first Palm Sunday, those other little children of God found joy in waving palm branches and in singing loud hosannas to His beloved Son as King of kings and Lord of lords. Thus we knew that Jesus had come to Umri, for He had dispelled all the spiritual darkness.

*   *   *

This morning, what does Palm Sunday mean to you? Does it mean more than the formal celebration of an event in the hoary past of the Christian faith? Indeed, Palm Sunday ought to mean vastly more to everyone here. It represents a tremendous issue that is alive today. Almost twenty centuries after Jesus rode into Jerusalem to claim full allegiance as King over all men everywhere, He stands in our midst today. He enters into our town, our church, our marketplace, our shops and our fields, our homes, and our inmost selves.

Today He "looks round about on all things." If anywhere He finds disorder, He traces it to rebellion against His Kingship, rebellion deep within our hearts. If you accept the issue honestly, at the sacrifice of all worldliness and fickleness, all self-righteousness and prejudice; if with childlike trust in Him as Lord and Saviour, you accept His full reign over every area of your inner being and your outer life, then He will cleanse the temple in your soul, and thus set it free for its intended service to God and men.

The Lord grant to every reader that this may be the meaning of Palm Sunday.

Aired February 15, 1946.
Mutual Broadcasting System,
"Faith in Our Time" series

"I Need a Chart"

"I Need a Chart!" Such was the title of a brief article my eye fell upon not long since. The author, I discovered, was a young naval officer, an old-time friend of mine. Of course I was interested.

This article related the plight of a mine sweeper in dangerous Puget Sound without a chart of the channel. The pilot radioed the naval base, "I need a chart!"

Mankind today is on that lost ship, with hidden dangers lurking on every side, and urgently calls for a chart by which to find the harbor. Our age is bewildered. Man has lost his sense of direction. Yesterday he confidently thought he could steer his own course, but today world-shaking events have left him confused and dismayed. His heart now fails him for fear. To him it seems that from the dark shore of the eternity that is past he has been set adrift on the ocean of time with no pilot to guide or star to cheer. Driving blindly before the storm, he awaits the inevitable doom. Confusing lights flicker in the distance, and siren voices call from the darkness — but what can he trust? Is there a way through the maze of life's channel to a safe harbor?

The truth we declare this morning is that God

has given man the chart, His written Word, to show man the way, the truth, and the life in Jesus Christ, the Incarnate Word.

Yes, in the Bible we have a chart, a guidebook which is never out-of-date. Ordinary guidebooks rapidly become obsolete and the cause of disaster when we follow them. How many of us at some time or other have come to grief because we have tried to follow an outdated railway guide? And this, notwithstanding the railroad company's plain warning that the published schedule is "subject to change without notice," that it has been revised to a date long past, and that the railroad "will not be responsible for errors in timetables, inconvenience, or damage resulting from delayed trains or failure to make connections."

But friend, the Bible is not dated! It was the safe guide of our fathers in the yesterdays; it directs us plainly today; our children tomorrow may fully rely upon its directions. We do not follow this chart at our own risk — it is the sure Word of God.

This chart, the Bible, is easily understood. How difficult ofttimes are man-made schedules! On occasion even those of us who travel much by train miss our way because we have misread the guidebook. But no great skill or learning is required to read from the Bible the basic relationships of life having to do with our right conduct toward our fellows here and our getting to heaven hereafter.

> There is a Book, who runs may read,
>   Which heavenly truth imparts,
> And all the lore its scholars need,
>   Pure eyes and Christian hearts.

And yet who can fathom this Book? Simple as it is in life's fundamentals, none of us will ever plumb its depths nor exhaust its treasure. What Matthew Henry said of a section of this Book may truly be said of all: In it are shallows where lambs may safely wade, deeps where elephants drown.

Whittier, the Quaker poet, paid tribute to the profound simplicity of this Book in these memorable lines:

> We search the world for truth; we cull
> The good, the pure, the beautiful
> From graven stone and written scroll,
> From all old flower-fields of the soul;
> And, weary seekers of the best,
> We come back laden from our quest,
> To find that all the sages said
> Is in the Book our mothers read.

Michael Faraday was a great scientist and a devout Christian. A friend found him in his study one day, arms crossed over his Bible and tears streaming down his face. In alarm the friend asked, "Dr. Faraday, what's the matter? Are you ill?" This great, wise, and good man answered, "Oh, no! But why, oh, why will men and women go astray when they have a Book like this to guide them?"

And we ask that question this morning: In all the welter of voices today, the confusion of tongues crying "Lo, here!" and "Lo, there!" why does man go astray when he may turn to this sure guide, the Word of God? This Book answers the cry of Job, "Oh that I knew where I might find him!" and the troubled question of doubting Thomas, "How can we know the way?" Here is man's chart!

But there are those who would not have it so. There are those who say that the Bible is not God's Word to man but only man's best word about God; that we have in the Bible merely the record of the best that man has ever known or felt about the true, the beautiful, the good. In my university days I asked one, supposedly a spiritual guide of students but who taught this view of the Bible, if we then must not expect some day another Bible — a nobler statement of man's quest for the ideal, a better word about God than man has yet uttered. He answered that we will never have another Bible just as there will never be another Milton or Shakespeare; but, he added, we may certainly expect nobler words about God than those given us by men of old in the book we call the Bible.

Lost indeed are we if the Bible is only man's word — if it is merely the mariner's log, the record of the bewildered sailor's blind sailing in quest of the harbor. But, thank God! this Book, the Bible, is the mariner's chart by which he may safely steer his course to the harbor.

The young naval officer, whose article ''I Need a Chart!'' gave us our morning's theme, closed his story with this testimony:

> I have found the chart in God's Word which clearly shows the port of destination and indicates the course to reach it. I have found this chart infallible and recommend it to any human craft which might ''need a chart.''

May those to whom this message comes this morning likewise turn to God's Word and with this young man take the Bible as the chart of life here that it may lead them on to eternal life hereafter.

In closing, I leave with you these soul-sustaining portions of God's Word by the pen of the Psalmist, who long ago made God's law and precepts his daily guide:

Wherewithal shall a young man cleanse his way? By taking heed thereto according to thy word. . . . Thy word have I hid in mine heart, that I might not sin against thee. . . . I will delight myself in thy statutes: I will not forget thy word. . . . Teach me, O Lord, the way of thy statutes; and I shall keep it unto the end. . . . So shall I keep thy law continually for ever and ever. And I will walk at liberty: for I seek thy precepts. . . . The law of thy mouth is better unto me than thousands of gold and silver. . . . O how love I thy law! It is my meditation all the day. . . . Through thy precepts I get understanding: therefore I hate every false way. Thy word is a lamp unto my feet, and a light unto my path.

Selections from Psalm 119

Aired September 17, 1950.
Columbia's Church of the Air (CBS).

God's Answer to Man's Hunger

And Jesus said unto them, I am the bread of life: he that cometh to me shall never hunger; and he that believeth on me shall never thirst.   John 6:35

Emerson once wrote that the health of a man is an equality of inlet and outlet, a balance of gathering and giving; and that any hoarding means tumor and disease. Jesus clearly taught this truth in His account of the rich farmer and his goods and his barns. As this man walked forth on his fertile acres and beheld the promise of a plentiful harvest, he was perplexed because his barns were already bursting with the bounty of previous harvests. "What shall I do" he asked, "because I have no room where to bestow my fruits? And he said, This will I do: I will pull down my barns, and build greater; and there will I bestow all my fruits and my goods. And I will say to my soul, Soul, thou hast much goods laid up for many years; take thine ease, eat, drink, and be merry."

This man thought nothing of outlet, only of inlet; nothing of giving, only of gathering. Eleven times in these few words he used the perpendicular pronoun

"I" and its possessive "my." How small and impoverished is the life hedged about by self! This man was already dead, spiritually dead — for he had choked to death on the good gifts of God which he would not share. And God said to him, "Thou fool, this night thy soul shall be required of thee. Then whose shall these things be that thou hast gathered?"

Yes, the miser, the glutton, the greedy must one day let go their goods which will at last be distributed even as the grim reaper gathers their poor, shriveled souls.

Many are the modern versions of this story of the rich farmer, the story of multitudes who would gain the whole world at the cost of their souls. Robert Service, poet of the Klondike, speaks their disillusionment in these familiar lines:

> I wanted the gold, and I sought it;
>   I scrabbled and mucked like a slave.
> Was it famine or scurvy — I fought it;
>   I hurled my youth into a grave.
>
> I wanted the gold, and I got it —
>   Came out with a fortune last fall —
> Yet somehow life's not what I thought it,
>   And somehow the gold isn't all.

Goods can never satisfy the hunger of man's heart. Moody, that great evangelist of an earlier generation, once said that a man's soul is bigger than this world; to pour the whole world into a man's soul is to leave that soul still empty. And may we add, so vast is the soul of man that the world rattles about in its resounding emptiness.

51

As disillusionment comes to individuals who seek satisfaction in material things, so is it with nations. Only a few generations have passed since our pioneering fathers set their energies to the task of subduing this continent; today, America is ours, but how greatly changed by the courage and industry and faith of those who have gone before us! Once-virgin prairies now yield bountiful harvests. Primeval forests have given way to teeming cities, quiet hamlets, lonely farmsteads. Rivers which through millenniums flowed on in primitive quiet now carry the fruit of forest and field and factory, and drive the wheels of commerce and industry. Railroads as ribbons of steel interlace our many commonwealths, while threads of steel flash our words around the world. Even the highways of the clouds are our thoroughfare, and the thunder-galleries of the heavens are our speaking-tube. And now even the atom has surrendered its secret of power by which we may control vast new areas of nature — if first we learn to control ourselves.

History has clearly written the record that the noontide of man's triumph over the material order is the fading twilight of the spiritual. When man is richest, then is he poorest — such is the paradox of prosperity. Conquest of the material world has not brought satisfaction of his deepest hunger. He finds not in wealth or power or pleasure the fullness of life he seeks. How truly wrote the wise man of old that he who ruleth his spirit is better than he who taketh a city. Man has taken cities; he has conquered his environment, but he has not mastered the world within. And anarchy there prevails.

Attempting to quiet life's hunger by feeding the soul the husks of material plenty, or by narcotizing it with sensual pleasure, or by intoxicating it with delirious passion is to live on life's lowest levels, forgetting that man is overbuilt for this world and that, in the sublime phrasing of the chaplain of my college days, "we are built for the universe, for eternity, and for God; and out and on and up into that heritage the normal living heart is ever pressing." And so the warning Jesus gave, "For what shall it profit a man, if he shall gain the world, and lose his own soul?"

What are we? Sons of God, or only superior animals? the crown of all creation or, as someone has said, merely "a boisterous bit of the organic scum of one small planet"? When we rob man of God and level him to the brute; when we convince man that he has no responsibility for his moral character but is only a puppet played by capricious fate, then chaos is the harvest, even a hell here on earth. Man cannot surrender faith in God and long retain belief in the significance of his own existence.

And so it is that a despairing modern wails, "I catch no meaning from all I have seen, and pass quite as I came, confused and dismayed." And a cynical modern flaunts his impious creed: the universe is a gigantic wheel in rapid revolution; man is a sick fly taking a dizzy ride on the wheel's whirling rim; religion is the fly's delusion that the wheel was constructed for the express purpose of giving him his ride. And a flippant modern calls man "an ape who chatters to himself of kinship with archangels while filthily he digs for groundnuts."

And a disillusioned modern laments his age, "the old age of thirty-five," recalling to us Lord Byron's entry in his journal on his thirty-third birthday, "I go to bed with a heaviness of heart at having lived so long and to so little purpose."

Byron here touches upon the secret of today's cynicism, disillusionment and despair. These come from living in the moment with no eternal purpose, accepting sensuous and material facts but denying spiritual and eternal values. Without an eternal purpose, life shrivels in all its four dimensions of length, breadth, height, and depth — shrinks to a mere point of time, the passing moment. From striving to press from each moment as it passes its last drop of pleasure comes premature age, "the old age of thirty-five" or, it may be, of twenty-five! Pathetic indeed are the life-weary, aged youth of our day, "having no hope, and without God in the world."

But is there no hope? The Apostle Paul gives the Christian answer in his letter to the Ephesian church in which he recalls the depth of moral degradation from which these Ephesian Christians had been lifted by the power of God's love:

> And you hath he quickened, who were dead in trespasses and sins; wherein in time past ye walked according to the course of this world, according to the prince of the power of the air, the spirit that now worketh in the children of disobedience: among whom also we all had our conversation in times past in the lusts of our flesh, fulfilling the desires of the flesh and of the mind; and were by nature the children of wrath, even as others.
>
> But God, who is rich in mercy, for his great love wherewith he loved us, even when we were dead in sins,

> hath quickened us together with Christ, (by grace are ye
> saved;) and hath raised us up together, and made us sit
> together in heavenly places in Christ Jesus: that in the
> ages to come he might show the exceeding riches of his
> grace in his kindness toward us through Christ Jesus.
>
> Ephesians 2:17

There is hope, then, because God cares. It was not to save whirling worlds from collision that God sent forth His Son into this universe, nor to hinge in space a new solar system. It was not to dig deep the Grand Canyon nor to pile high the Rockies or the Andes that God sent His Son to our small world, a speck in the great universe. But to bridge with His own Person that gulf of separation between man and his Creator, God sought out this planet and here, by the tragic sacrifice of himself in the Person of His Son, spanned heaven and earth to bring man back to himself.

Even in man's cynicism and despair God is seeking to draw man to himself to satisfy man's deepest heart hunger, his burning soul-thirst.

George Herbert explains man's restlessness apart from God in the following lines which have endured through three centuries:

> When God at first made man,
> Having a glass of blessings standing by;
> Let us (said He) pour on him all we can:
> Let the world's riches, which disperséd lie,
>   Contract into a span.
>
> So strength first made a way;
> Then beauty flowed, then wisdom, honour, pleasure:
> When almost all was out, God made a stay,
> Perceiving that alone of all His treasure
>   Rest in the bottom lay.

> For if I should (said He)
> Bestow this jewel also on My creature,
> He would adore My gifts instead of Me,
> And rest in Nature, not the God of Nature:
>   So both should losers be.
>
> Yet let him keep the rest
> But keep them with repining restlessness:
> Let him be rich and weary, that at least,
> If goodness lead him not, yet weariness
>   May toss him to My breast.

Yes, God made us for himself, then gave himself for us. Jesus Christ is God's gift to man, answering man's heart-cry in the words of our theme-passage, "I am the bread of life: he that cometh to me shall never hunger; and he that believeth on me shall never thirst."

Responding by faith to this promise, man becomes indeed a child of God, restored to the divine favor which sin had forfeited. This change is more than a mystical idealism stirring man to noble sentiments — it is vital fellowship with a Divine Person. This change is more than mental assent to Christian truth — it is life made dynamic by the indwelling Christ. This change is more than moral heroism straining for salvation through good works — it is childlike trust resting securely in a Father's love. The response of our faith to God goes deeper than our religious sentiments, our reasoning about truth, or our fullest purpose to do good. This faith is the response of our inmost, utmost self to the call of God uttered in unmistakable accents in Jesus Christ as our only Saviour.

The Prodigal Son made that simple response of

faith to the love of his father. Perishing with hunger in a far country, he came to himself and remembered that in his father's house even servants had bread and to spare. He arose and came to his father, confessing his sin, his waywardness, and his unworthiness to be a son, begging rather for employment as a hired servant. His father forgave and fed and clothed him, not as a servant under legal contract, but as a son under the favor of a father's love.

Some who have heard in this message today Christ's offer of bread for the hungry heart may be perishing of hunger in some far country of sin and pride and self-will. If you are such an one, with sincere purpose now say, "I will arise and go to my father"; and while you are yet a great way off, the Father's love revealed in Jesus Christ will meet you. Faith is that simple: coming to Christ, we are fed; believing on Christ, our thirst is quenched.

Thus God answers man's hunger. He did not make us with an infinite craving without providing its satisfaction. And with St. Augustine we exclaim, "Thou hast made us for Thyself, and we are restless until we find rest in Thee."

Given at the dedication
of the Greenville College Library.
An extraordinary care for fusing learning
and "passion for God and man" is shown.
Books, Marston argues, provide the shoulders
for the advance of civilization
and the growth of the Christin church.

"Bring . . . the Books"
(II Timothy 4:13)

Our announced subject is the phrasing of the Apostle Paul in his second recorded letter to his son in the gospel, Timothy, written from a Roman prison where Paul is awaiting his execution. Nearing the close of the letter, Paul reaches one of his heights of eloquence in his great valedictory:

> For I am now ready to be offered, and the time of my departure is at hand. I have fought a good fight, I have finished my course, I have kept the faith: henceforth there is laid up for me a crown of righteousness, which the Lord, the righteous judge, shall give me at that day.
>
> II Timothy 4:6-8

From this skyline Paul quickly drops to the practical and commonplace: "Do thy diligence to come shortly unto me," he says, explaining that except for Luke he is quite alone. Then he asks that Timothy perform a few chores for him:

> The cloak that I left at Troas with Carpus, when thou comest, bring with thee, and the books, but especially the parchments.
>
> II Timothy 4:13

What a human fragment is this! Paul asks for his

old overcoat which no doubt had accompanied him on many a perilous journey and is now needed to protect him against the chill of his dank Roman dungeon in the winter just ahead. The rigors of the approaching season are evidently in his mind, for later in the letter he urges, "Do thy diligence to come before winter" (II Timothy 4:21). But he craves for more than physical relief. He pleads for his library, no doubt a small one for a man of such wide travels and no fixed abode, but assuredly a most excellent one. What a rare book list a catalog of Paul's library would provide! And finally he adds, "but especially the parchments." What were these? Was his university diploma among them, signed by the famous Dr. Gamaliel? Perhaps his certificate of Roman citizenship? Or some rare manuscripts upon which Paul had been engaged in research? Even some sermon outlines or unfinished letters to the churches, half completed when Paul was hurried away from Troas under arrest? How Paul in his gloomy dungeon longed for the companionship of his books and manuscripts!

This man who would have his books with him the last months of his life was the greatest influence for the spread of Christianity in all the centuries of the early church. It was no accident or irrelevance that this pioneer missionary and church statesman was a man of learning, of culture, of books.

Books had played an important part in the Hebrew tradition in which Paul had been reared. Other than the sacred books of the Jews, comprising for us essentially the Old Testament, were other books of such significance that the Hebrew Scriptures refer to them not infrequently. Among these are *The Wars of the Lord, Chronicles of David, Acts of Solomon, Visions of Iddo, Samuel and the Kingdom.*

Among the bibliographic references found in the Old Testament, one writer lists Solomon's *Natural History,* his claim based probably on I Kings 4:33, which I quote with the verse preceding:

> And he [Solomon] spake three thousand proverbs: and his songs were a thousand and five. And he spake of trees, from the cedar tree that is in Lebanon even unto the hyssop that springeth out of the wall: he spake also of beasts, and of fowl, and of creeping things, and of fishes.
>
> I Kings 4:32-33

Nothing is said here of writing nor of a book, but since we have in the book of Proverbs nearly a third of the three thousand proverbs he spoke; and of the thousand and five songs he composed we have perhaps three in the book of Psalms and also the book called the Song of Solomon, we may reasonably infer that Solomon's discourses on nature were also recorded in a book.

If indeed Solomon did write a book on natural history, and if his authorship of Ecclesiastes be granted, these two books with his acknowledged authorship of Proverbs, some of the Psalms, and the Song of Solomon give him high rank as a versatile writer in such varied fields as science, philosophy, ethics, and poetry. Who, then, better than Solomon, could say, "of making many books there is no end, and much study is a weariness of the flesh?"

(Ecclesiastes 12:12)

Following Solomon and the division of his kingdom there came periods of decline in Judah with occasional and partial revival. Religious declension was accompanied by neglect of the great books of Hebrew tradition, and for a time even the Temple copy of the book of the Law, written by Moses, was lost. One of the dramatic episodes of sacred history is the finding of this lost book during the revival under the youthful and righteous king Josiah in the seventh century. After King Josiah had purged the land of idolatry he ordered the repair of the Temple. During the process of repair, the high priest found this precious but forgotten book, long lost in the accumulating debris of the abandoned and desolate house of the Lord.

There were not only authors and books in ancient time, but also libraries where books were collected and librarians who handled them according to system. Libraries developed in that land which was the cradle of the race more than four thousand years ago. At an early date Babylon was the center of learning and records, but by the middle of the seventh century B.C., Nineveh seems to have surpassed Babylon as a library center. Here a vast collection of records was assembled, and the books were classified, cataloged and indexed by title. Dewey is not as modern as we may think!

Two instances of library research are interestingly related in the Book of Ezra. The Samaritans reported to the Persian King, Smerdis, a usurper following the death of Cyrus, that the Jews were rebuilding their Temple in Jerusalem, and referred the King to "the book of the records" to confirm their charge that Jerusalem had been "a rebellious city, and hurtful unto kings." In his reply Smerdis said:

> The letter which ye sent unto us hath been plainly read before me. And I commanded and search hath been made, and it is found that this city of old time hath made insurrection against kings, and that rebellion and sedition have been made therein.   Ezra 4:18-19

And Smerdis ordered the rebuilding to stop.

But after the death of the usurper, Smerdis, the Jews renewed their work on the Temple and when challenged by their old enemies, the Samaritans, they answered that they were proceeding under the decree of Cyrus that the Temple be rebuilt. Darius, a legitimate successor, was now on the throne, and the Samaritans appealed to him, asking that he have a search made of "the king's treasure house, which is there at Babylon, whether it be so, that a decree was made of Cyrus the King to build their house of God at Jerusalem," and advise the inquiriers of his pleasure in the matter. But this time the Samaritans overreached in their appeal to historical research. Darius ordered search of the royal library and the decree of Cyrus was located. Darius then fully enforced the decree of Cyrus and the Temple was brought to quick completion.

Library research thus antedates the establishment of the Greenville College Memorial Library by a few years — twenty-five centuries in fact!

We have mentioned but a few incidents of concern for books in the tradition in which Paul had been educated, but we would note also that in the subsequent course of the Christian church, books and libraries played an important part. Chief of the books which concerned the early church and led to the writing of vast libraries were those which constitute our New Testament, thirteen or fourteen of which are from the pen of Paul himself.

We are told that as soon as church structures were built in the early church, libraries were established in them. Some of these libraries came to considerable importance. Eusebius, who wrote around A.D. 300, spoke of Bishop Alexander's library at Jerusalem as a storehouse of knowledge, admitting that he secured from it most of the material for his *Ecclesiastical History*. The library of Saint Sophia's at Constantinople had 100,000 volumes by A.D. 400.

During the Middle Ages the monasteries became repositories of books and manuscripts, and copying books became a chief employment of the monks prior to the invention of printing. These book treasures of the church formed the beginnings of the medieval universities and later the Renaissance drew upon them for some of its classic sources.

Nearly fifteen hundred years after Paul wrote to Timothy, asking him to bring to his Roman prison-home his books and parchments, a humble German miner sensed the stir of new mental life breaking up the stagnation of medieval Europe, and resolved that his son should be a scholar. When the lad was fourteen years old the father sent him away to school. Without money, this lad became a mendicant or "begging scholar" to secure his bread.

At eighteen, this boy, Martin Luther, went to the

University at Erfurth. In his last year here, shortly before his degree, while browsing in the library which was his delight, he discovered a rare book, the Bible. He recognized in it fragments used in church worship, and thrilled as he turned its pages — pages of the very Word of God, complete! His eyes lingered on the moving story of Hannah and Samuel. (Yes — bring the books! Samuel was raised among them, no doubt, in the house of the Lord!)

Graduated with honors but seeking a perfection he keenly realized he lacked, against his father's will he turned from teaching and law to the priesthood. He entered an Augustinian monastery, taking with him all his possessions, two books — and they, one of them at least, a strange choice! These were *Virgil* and *Plautus*.

But he found no peace in the monastery. Then came the occasion when God spoke to him — according to tradition, as he was mounting Pilate's stair on his knees in Rome — spoke to him from that Book he found in his university days, saying in the words of Paul to the Romans, "The just shall live by faith."

Martin Luther, throughout the subsequent years as the Great Reformer, carried with him "the books," bringing to the destruction of error the light of his great learning. Even when excommunicated and in exile in the forest castle, he brought *The Book* from its tomb of the dead languages to life in the tongue of German peasants. Without books, Luther never would have become the Great Reformer; without books, he would have lived and died a simple German peasant.

Two centuries after Luther, John Wesley, another man of books, a graduate and fellow of Oxford who long had sought justification by works as had Luther, while hearing *Luther's Preface to Paul's Letter to the Romans,* accepted Christ as his justification by faith, and his heart was strangely warmed.

What a succession: Paul through his Roman letter reached the heart of Martin Luther; and Luther, commenting on that letter, reached the heart of John Wesley. And all three of them — Paul, Luther, Wesley — men of books!

Wesley's heartwarming in 1738 led to the establishment of a school at Kingswood the following year. In 1756, addressing the clergy, and underscoring his concern for books, Wesley outlined the desirable qualifications of the minister to include the study of history, geography, logic, metaphysics, natural science, geometry, the Scriptures in both English and their original languages, and the manners of a gentleman; for the clergyman, said Wesley, should exhibit "all the courtesy of a gentleman, joined with the correctness of a scholar."

Early Methodism's influence upon learning was amazing. Lay preachers, many converted late in life who had not received the benefits of a formal education but were untutored, simple tradesfolk and artisans, became Greek and Hebrew scholars. This they achieved by taking with them on their itinerant duties "the books."

Less than a century after Wesley's heartwarming, a revival meeting in Middletown, Connecticut, under the leadership of that remarkable physician,

Dr. John Wesley Redfield, greatly stirred a freshman in Wesleyan University. That freshman was Benjamin Titus Roberts who later graduated from Wesleyan and shortly became a prominent young preacher in the Western New York area. He too brought with him "the books," and when Providence thrust upon him the burden of establishing another Methodist communion, one of his first steps, as had been Wesley's, was the founding of a school. Six years after the new denomination was organized, this revered founder-bishop of Free Methodism gave heed to "the books" and established what now is known as Roberts Wesleyan College. Other institutions followed, and nearly sixty years ago this college was founded.

In that excellent little book, *Fishers of Men,* Bishop Roberts follows Wesley's emphasis on books in exhorting ministers to the study of the Scriptures in Hebrew and Greek, in the study of science, literature, history, and mathematics; and adds, "In short, every branch of human knowledge can be used to advantage in the work of winning souls to God." Again he says:

> The gospel has always been the friend of learning, and they who would labor with success to diffuse its blessings must avail themselves of their opportunties to acquire useful knowledge.

Stevens, historian of Methodism, records that "Methodism was cradled in a university." Bishop Wilson T. Hogue, the founder-president of Greenville College and historian of Free Methodism, states:

The men who were chiefly instrumental in founding the Free Methodist Church were for the most part men who had been trained in colleges and universities. They were not the men lightly to esteem intellectual training, or to suppose that, in the founding of His kingdom, God ever places a premium upon ignorance.

Paul, Luther, Wesley, Roberts — mighty preachers of the gospel, brought to the service of religion both their natural gifts and their vast learning from books, fused to a white heat by the flame of their passion for God and man.

We have tried to relate this library, which today we dedicate, to the great Hebrew-Christian tradition, entwining millenniums of history. The church's pioneering in letters and libraries likewise relates that tradition closely to the development of culture and learning in general; but we do not pause here to trace their connections, so commonly recognized. Now we briefly examine the meaning of learning and of books to human history.

Years ago we had a ten-year-old boy in our home, and I recall his monotonously droning this bit of verse he was memorizing for his English class —

> Suppose the world were yet too young —
>   Men had not thought of books;
> Suppose there were no libraries,
>   No cozy reading nooks;
> Suppose — it is too horrible
>   To think it might be true:
> On rainy days and wintry nights
>   What would a fellow do?

In some small way, these lines express the importance to a child of the experiences of the race stored in books for our enjoyment. An empty world, indeed, were there no books for "rainy days and wintry nights."

But far greater would be the tragedy if the human race should suddenly lose every trace of the past recorded on memory's page through learning. Graham Wallas in *Our Social Heritage* speculates on what would happen to civilization if a comet should so strike our planet that every human being would instantly lose all knowledge and all habits acquired from past generations, while retaining full powers of mind — memory, reason, inventiveness, and the like. Wallas predicts these consequences:

> In thirty days nine-tenths of the inhabitants of our larger cities such as London, New York, and Chicago would be dead;
>
> In six months ninety-nine percent of the remainder would perish;
>
> There would be no language to express thought, and consequently thought itself would be sketchy and blurred;
>
> Within a few years man would almost entirely vanish from northern and temperate regions; the white race would perish, and only a few of southern races would survive in the tropics to begin again the slow pace toward a new civilization;
>
> Only after thousands of years would appear the rudiments of a new social heritage with a crude language, simple practices of animal husbandry, the rudiments of agriculture, and the like.

Whether or not Wallas is correct in details he is right in his essential point which is *man's tremendous dependence upon learning from the past.*

With such catastrophe as here depicted for the human race should it lose all learning from the past, contrast what would happen in ape society if the apes of the jungle should suddenly forget everything they have learned from the past. What would then happen? Nothing!

Why the difference? The orders of creatures below man must start anew each generation. At birth they are pretty well equipped with a nervous mechanism ready to function adequately in the simple and rather fixed patterns by which they must live, depending little upon learning from the past. The experience of the race stored in books has no place in their life preparation. But man stands upon the shoulders of the race, supreme as a creature with capacity to learn. And because man must learn from the past if he is to live, nature has provided him a prolonged period of growth and immaturity in which to gain a measure of mastery of the essential habits and ideas and ideals of the race.

Through books, then, the past shuttles its woof through the warp of time and significantly shapes the pattern of present and future. Isaiah, that courtly prophet of the eighth century B.C., declared the purpose of books to perpetuate the experience of nations for subsequent times when he urged with reference to the sins of his people:

> Now go, write it before them on a tablet, and note it in a book, that it may be for the time to come for ever and ever. Isaiah 30:8

And long before Isaiah (if we accept the antiquity of Job), that dramatic figure of religious history declared his desire to write the declaration of his triumphant faith in a book of stone to be read to the end of time:

Oh that my words were now written! Oh that they were printed in a book! That they were graven with an iron pen and lead in the rock for ever!   Job 19:23-24

The desires of both Isaiah and Job are surely fulfilled in the eternity of that Word which records their words.

Here are further words about books by men of more recent time:

Books are the legacies that a great genius leaves to mankind, which are delivered from generation to generation, as presents to the posterity of those yet unborn.   Addison, in *The Spectator*

God be thanked for books. They are the voices of distant lands and the dead, and make us heirs of the spiritual life of past ages.   Wm. E. Channing

For books are more than books, they are the life,
The very heart and core of ages past,
The reason why men lived and worked and died,
The essence and quintessence of their lives.
                                                    Amy Lowell

Old books are books of the world's youth, and new books are fruits of its age.   O. W. Holmes

A great library contains the diary of the race.
                                                    George Dawson

Because of man's ability to learn from the treasured experiences of the race stored in books, he is set free from the bondage of circumstance. Peary, that Arctic explorer of the last generation when no radio enlarged the explorer's contacts with humankind, testified that the well-read man could withstand the rigors of the north with greater mental poise and health than the uneducated. Mile on mile of snow and icy waste; months on end beyond the reach of civilization; long, long days within the Arctic Circle, and then again interminable nights — how sordidly dreary such a world! But the man of books who commands the rich heritage of the ages, when cut off from human society and buried in desolation, has within a kingdom of spiritual resources upon which to draw. He lives with the poets and artists and historians; he sojourns in distant places and dwells in fairer climes. He overleaps the boundaries of geography to make the universe his home; he breaks the lockstep of time and joins himself to eternity.

In the poem called "Goshen!" Edgar Frank eloquently sets forth the freedom books bring:

> "How can you live in Goshen?"
> Said a friend from afar,
> "This wretched country town
> Where folks talk little things all year,
> And plant their cabbage by the moon!"
>
> Said I:
> "I do not live in Goshen, —
> I eat here, sleep here, work here;
> I live in Greece,
> Where Plato taught,
> And Phidias carved,
> And Epictetus wrote.
> I dwell in Italy,
> Where Michael Angelo wrought
> In color, form and mass;
> Where Cicero penned immortal lines,
> And Dante sang undying songs.
> Think not my life is small

> Because you see a puny place;
> I have my books; I have my dreams;
> A thousand souls have left for me
> Enchantment that transcends
> Both time and place.
> And so I live in Paradise,
> Not here."

The part that learning plays in the adjustment of man to a complex world order we have noted and have distinguished man from the brute by his ability to profit by racial experience stored in books. I would leave with you a further word.

More crucial than this distinction in terms of learning is that quality in man by which he is capable of a divine discontent which never disturbs the brute. The former distinction between man and brute is relative, for animals after all do learn. This distinction is absolute, for only man can seek or shun God.

Perhaps some do not hold that this distinction is an advantage in man's favor. Evidently Walt Whitman did not, for he wrote these lines and called them poetry:

> I think I could return and live with animals, they are so
>   placid and self-contained;
> I stand and look at them long and long.
> They do not sweat and whine about their condition;
> They do not lie awake in the dark and weep for their sins;
> They do not make me sick discussing their duty to God;
> Not one is dissatisfied —

But thank God for this divine discontent! Thank God you are human and lie awake, weeping for your sins! Thank God for an insatiate longing for Him and a capacity to know Him which transcends all learning! For God has not made us with an infinite craving without providing its satisfaction. God has not left man to grope his way alone in the light of human intellect to the discovery of saving truth, as Wallas's survivors of an imagined world catastrophe must make their slow and painful way of social evolution to the rudiments of a new civilization. The saving truth of God is not reached in the ordinary give-and-take of experience through life or books. In the book of Job, Elihu says to his elders:

> Days should speak, and multitude of years should teach wisdom. But there is a spirit in man: and the inspiration of the Almighty giveth them understanding.
> Job 32:7-8

Elihu has kept silence out of respect for the years and greater experience of his companions, but finally he can no longer hold his peace. Life experience, he says here, should count for something in acquiring wisdom. Yes, trial-and-error has its learning value. But man is capable of something higher than learning by experience. Man is more than mind — he is also spirit. Therefore, God can speak to man, quickening his understanding to spiritual insight as the truth of revelation grips him.

Our closing word, then, refers to the Word, the revelation of God in the Incarnate Word made real to us by the Spirit's application to heart and conscience of the written Word.

This beautiful library which we have met to dedicate betrays its tradition of millenniums and fails its mission to this and coming generations unless at its center is the Living Word. Those who direct youthful minds to its treasures must trace the myriad flashing rays of universal truth to that Word as central sun.

> We search the world for truth. We cull
> The good, the true, the beautiful
> From graven stone and written scroll,
> From all old flower-fields of the soul;
> And, weary seekers of the best,
> We come back laden from our quest,
> To find that all the sages said
> Is in the Book our mothers read.
>
> John Greenleaf Whittier

Rebels Against the Yoke

> Come unto me, all ye that labor and are heavy laden, and I will give you rest. Take my yoke upon you, and learn of me; for I am meek and lowly in heart: and ye shall find rest unto your souls. For my yoke is easy, and my burden is light.
>
> Matthew 11:28-30

In these gracious words our Lord calls upon those who are world-weary and yoke-galled by sin to share His gentle yoke and learn to live under the loving restraints of His teaching.

But we in America these recent years have been rebels against the yoke. We have turned away from that learning which is constrained by the patterns of righteousness and truth revealed in the Word of God and tested by centuries of human history. Our watchword has been *freedom,* and by freedom we have meant irresponsibility, and ofttimes license. We have desired no yoke, and until yesterday we have thought we could escape its galling restraint. But now we are beginning to question if, after all, we like this yokeless freedom.

The "new morality," which has now flowed into full bloom from the seed-sowing of nineteenth-century naturalism, has falsely assumed the innate rightness of human nature, if not its goodness.

75

According to the "new morality," man needs no yoke of restraint; let him be true to his own nature and he will grow into sweetness and light. Because of this doctrine, the contrary concept of sin has rapidly become obsolete, and leaders of the "new morality" are definitely seeking to eradicate from human experience the consciousness of sin. Permit one illustration:

An advocate of the "new morality" is Dora Russell, one-time wife of philosopher Bertrand Russell of England, who shares her former husband's widely known views on sex morals. Dora Russell has written a book, published in this country, which American youth finds easy and interesting reading. Its title, *The Right to Be Happy,* should carry as subtitle, "No Obligation to Be Right," for the book advocates the release of men and women from the yoke of our basic sex morality; and to secure that release the author says, "The idea of sin must be banished."

Under the "new morality," standards have been leveled, patterns have been blurred, restraints have been let go. With fading of our consciousness of sin, sin itself has rapidly increased in prevalence and virulence. Judged both by the prevalence of sin and man's declining sense of sin, this is indeed a pagan age.

Oh, yes, 'tis true our fathers sinned; and at certain periods on the frontier of American pioneering our fathers may have sinned to the same or greater excess. But, they sinned with a consciousness of guilt and the smart of outraged ideals, whereas the children of this age indulge without scruple, and even as George Eliot wrote of Tito in *Romola,* with "lips that lie with a dimpled smile, eyes with a gleam that no infamy dulls, a conscience that rises from lust and murder without a haggard look."

Under the guidance of the "new morality," a "new education" has likewise developed during recent years. Grounded likewise in the doctrine of nature's rightness, the "new education" focalizes the learner and his experience as the factors of quite exclusive pedagogical concern. Therefore it sets the goal, both of education and of life, by selfish interests rather than by the glory of God or the good of fellow man. Such "yokeless" learning relaxes the tension between duty and interest by the strangulation of the ideal of duty. Inner conflict subsides in our youth under this program, not through conquest of self in submission to the yoke of duty, but through unresisting surrender of duty to selfishness. Again as in the days of the Greek Sophists, man — the individual man — becomes the measure of all things; what he wants, it is right he should have — if he can wrest it from others; what he believes, is true — if he can outwit his rival in debate.

A few years ago a panel of guest speakers at an educational conference sponsored by a great university discussed the social responsibility of the public school. The most vociferous members of the group contended for education in terms of strictly contemporary social values centering about the child's immediate experience. These wanted no yoke of the past to constrain our children's learning; no restraints of ideals, time-tested in racial experience. . . .

The outcome of "yokeless" learning has recently been pointed out by Dr. Alfred Adler of the University of Chicago. Dr. Adler describes today's youth as lacking loyalties and having no moral philosophy because of America's patternless or "yokeless" education. His criticism gains sharper point by Dorothy Thompson's column, likewise of an October date, reporting a fireside chat with four graduates of eastern universities who represent the products of America's best social and intellectual traditions. These boys bitterly lamented that their education had broken their beliefs in positive values, had weakened their faith in their country, had robbed them of their enthusiasms, had cut them loose from their moorings and set them adrift with no controls or guides. All this in consequence of learning without a yoke!

But it was several years ago that the late distinguished scholar, Professor William Shorey, discerned the situation in higher education and was alarmed for the outcome of rejecting the yoke. He declared then that an ambitious young professor could safely in his classroom attack Christianity, the Constitution of the United States, chastity, marriage, and private property; but he must not condemn obscene literature nor oppose the teaching of materialism lest he be guilty of intolerance!

In religion, likewise, America has rebelled against the yoke. Only a few months ago I attended the Protestant church council of a great state conference on social work. About the speakers' table at the dinner session sat several clergymen. The principal speaker of the evening, a layman, was a rather prominent administrator of a school for delinquent boys. This man raised the question, "What is the purpose of a sermon?" One preacher in the circle answered, "To instruct." "No!" the big man objected, "The preacher has no right trying to indoctrinate me. My beliefs are as valid as his." Then, I ventured an answer: "The sermon should disturb." But this likewise the speaker rejected. "The purpose of a sermon," he said, "is to soothe."

But the great Apostle Paul, foreseeing the time when men would demand religion without a yoke, exhorted his young colleague, Timothy, so to preach as both to instruct and disturb. Hear his words: "I adjure you to preach the word; keep at it in season and out of season, refuting, checking, and exhorting men; never lose patience with them, and never give up your teaching, for the time will come when people will decline to be taught sound doctrine and will accumulate teachers to suit themselves and tickle their own fancy" (II Timothy 4:2-3, Moffatt).

Most of this audience can recall when the moral thinking of the nation very largely followed the patterns of the Sunday pulpit, the religious press, and the little red schoolhouse, with the family circle the integrating element of these patterns. Today, the little red schoolhouse is gone. The family circle has been broken into fragmentary arcs by the automobile, the bridge club, and the movie. The Sunday paper has smothered to suffocation the church weekly and the Sunday-school paper. The Sunday pulpit for most Americans is that narrow, unused sector of the radio dial across which skilled fingers twirl the program selector to bring in the day's baseball game, the latest vaudeville gag, a breathtaking drama, or a symphony. And the best program may have as sponsor the greatest enemy of character!

Increasingly dominant likewise is the motion picture. A group of New England school principals, answering a questionnaire which asked which agency exerts the greatest character-forming influence — school, church, or home — in a strong majority scratched out all three and wrote in, "The movies."

Yes, enemies of the yoke have come in like a raging flood, obliterating old patterns of right and wrong and leveling old standards. Home, church, and school, our former bulwarks, have in large measure lost their effectiveness in crumbling disintegration under the assaults of the "new morality."

Our big problem today — perhaps our biggest — is youth adrift on the tempestuous sea of moral individualism, chart blurred by the compromises of its elders, and compass desensitized to the north pole of unchanging truth and swinging impulsively to every movement of the ship itself. Thus adrift without controls, youth drives madly before the gale under the intoxicating delusion that it is free.

But the vaunted freedom of this age is not freedom at all, but that centrifugal disorganization which follows upon the severing of life's stabilizing controls. Life needs a guiding pattern, the directing restraints of banks for its energies. The outcome of living without patterns is capricious chaos, "a dizzy whirl about a central emptiness." Today's alleged self-expression is that careening, breathtaking moment which spans the automobile's lurch from the driver's control and the highway to the blazing and twisted wreckage at the foot of the embankment. Paradoxical as it seems, if life is to achieve freedom it must submit to the yoke.

Because America has rebelled against the yoke, throwing off the moral and spiritual guides of Christian patterns, she is now a fallow but fertile field, prepared by the tolerance of indifference to receive the seed of pagan propaganda from Europe's weed patch. During the past generation or more we have taken for granted the Christian basis of our culture, indolently resting in the false security of merely nominal Christianity while consuming our Christian heritage without replacements. Thus, paganism has stolen upon us unawares — a soft, indulgent, yokeless idolatry of self which is deaf to the challenge of the heroic and the ideal.

But reaction tends to follow license. A people that in one generation spurns the yoke that would hold it to eternal values, in a later generation may turn from its aimless wanderings to throw itself before false gods. Unless America yields again and speedily to the yoke of Christ, paganism will shortly spawn, from our present idolatry of self, the cruel idolatry of organized human power elevated to the throne of God. Sooner or later human nature becomes surfeited with self and cries out for something bigger than self to worship.

Do you doubt this? Then look upon the rapidly shifting panorama of today's old-world crises. Whereas America's god still is self, other nations have reached that reactionary stage of paganism in which base loyalties and sacrificing devotion to false heroes have blazed to life in the human breast. Humanity clamoring for a yoke! Someone has pointed out the disturbing fact that Christianity no longer has its crusaders, its fanatics, its martyrs; such now are found only in the ranks of the new paganism. Yes, old-world paganism has gone militant, its right arm holding aloft the nazi-fascist god of tribalism while its left supports the communist god of humanism; and both are now merging into Moloch, god of destruction and the hard taskmaster of life whose lust for human blood is never sated.

The ringing call of militant paganism has peculiar power to stir youth to rebellion against the frustration and deadening paralysis of self-idolatry. Militant paganism the world around is essentially a youth movement. Youth is idealistic, or at least is easily attracted to idealism when it craves a cause demanding sacrifice. Dr. Daniel Poling has reported that on his world tour on behalf of youth four or five years ago, he found youth everywhere on the march — marching for some cause that youth felt was bigger than self. Everywhere he went youth was asking, "Isn't there something better than life? the cause? the nation?" Again and again in one form or another, youth asked him the question, "What will a man die for?"

How can we explain this quest of youth for a cause — yes, for a yoke! A few weeks ago I heard E. Stanley Jones tell a youth group, "Do as you like and you will not like what you do; express yourself and you will not like the self you express." Why is this?

We find the answer in the nature of the "self." Properly speaking, a "self" is not a loose aggregation of impulses, caprices, and passions flying at cross purposes. A "self" is the direction of energy within channels, and is neither its destructive dissipation in a flood nor its stagnation in a swamp. For the realization of his true "self," man's energies must have banks to restrain and direct them. Reverting to the figure of our lesson, man best realizes himself as free by submitting himself to the restraints of a yoke. Clearly did the psalmist grasp this truth of freedom through law, of liberty under the yoke, in these lines: "So shall I keep thy law continually for ever and ever. And I will walk at liberty: for I seek thy precepts" (Psalm 119:44, 45).

But without the restraints of law, of fixed principles of conduct, insecurity and fear grip man; he is lost, unable to find himself because he has no organizing center to give meaning to life. Having energies, but no tracks upon which these energies may run, he experiences frustration if not despair or panic.

And so it happens that modern youth, product of the "new morality" and the "new education," having no convictions, knowing no purpose and therefore lacking inner security, too often in despair turns to the yoke that means galling bondage rather than the rest of freedom. Dorothy Thompson, in the column already mentioned, which reports her interview with four young university graduates, points out that it was of just such rudderless youth in quest of a faith and a cause that Hitler took advantage. And so today, Hitler speaks and millions of youth leap to his call! He has given German youth a cause and tracks for their energies. And Dr. Aubrey, discussing the radical skepticism of this century which suspects, if it doesn't reject, all convictions, says that modern sophisticates, "yearning for stability and unable to find it within . . . will submit to the dictator who can artificially create it from without." And this, he claims is why fascism is possible even to intellectuals. (E. E. Aubrey, "What Is New in the Religious Problem of the Twentieth Century," *Christian Education,* April 1935.)

The militant paganism that has enlisted the youth of the world is even now bidding for America's youth. Can the Christian church outbid this strenuous paganism? Certainly not with easy concessions to youth's assumed love of self such as the church has been offering these many years in a despairing effort to compete with selfish paganism. The church is rapidly losing its youth-appeal at this very point of excessive pampering, just as selfish paganism elsewhere has yielded to militant paganism.

Christian America should blush at the words of a Russian youth, reported by Bishop Cushman — blush that it has failed to challenge American youth for Christ as Stalin has challenged Russian youth for Moloch! Dr. Cushman relates that when traveling in Russia, his group encountered a member of the organization of "godless" youth who said, "Our organization is fighting three things: sex impurity, liquor, and tobacco." Someone asked, "Why are you fighting these things?" The young atheist answered, "We young people can't afford to waste our money or our health when we have on our hands the job of making a new Russia" (Ralph S. Cushman, *I Have a Stewardship,* Abingdon, 1939). And Dr. Arnold Toynbee has somewhere pointed out that it is "by making large demands on human nature, and not by offering people the license to do as they like and live at their ease, that the postwar paganism has been winning its masses of converts."

But, will American youth respond to the challenge of yokeship with Christ? It will, if the church sincerely presents that challenge. Youth looks to us to point the way.

Witness the recent editorial in the *Daily Iowan,* student newspaper of the University of Iowa. This half-page spread was addressed as "An Open Letter to the Faculty and Administration" under the caption, *Take Us Back to Solid Ground.* The editorial reads in part: "We aren't living within our means, and we followed your example. We are afraid of hard work; you never taught us to love it. We can't accept responsibility; you couldn't before us. We don't know the meaning of discipline; you didn't discipline us. . . . We want constant training in the constant things of life. . . . We want to get our teeth into something vibrant and alive, something permanent, something which ties the present to the *truths* of a glorious past. We want discipline in the job of living."

Nor is this plea from one university campus the sole evidence that American youth is groping for a yoke.

Harpers (February 1941) carried a significant article by Doris Drucker, "Authority for Our

Children," reporting the results of a survey of college youth across the nation which shows that young people today desire guidance, authority, and the knowledge of right and wrong. According to this survey, youth itself considers that it has had too little guidance from the school, the church, and the home. These young people hold the home especially responsible for the authority they needed but didn't get. The author comments that perhaps for the first time in modern history a youth generation clamors not for more freedom, "but wants less freedom and more security."

Yes, in clearly discernible measure American youth is beginning to ask for a yoke, and in the months and years just ahead of us youth will find and accept some yoke, some cause which will challenge it to heavy sacrifice. To win against Moloch, the church must sound to youth a greater challenge, the challenge of the Cross which means yokeship with Christ.

> There is a tide in the affairs of men,
> Which taken at the flood, leads on to fortune.

The tide of youth's loyalty has turned, and soon will be at the flood. Can we capture that loyalty for Christ? Youth is now "ready for great dedications," and we must win youth to Christ's yoke today; tomorrow may be too late.

Evangelical Christianity in a Pagan Age

Events of world-shaking import have transpired since last we assembled in an annual convention. Then we were in the midst of organized world conflict. The week following our Chicago meeting came peace in Europe. We rejoiced and gave thanks unto God. But our joy was not complete. The enemy in the Pacific still engaged millions of our boys, and the heavy sacrifice of life and health continued long months.

Then in late summer came our sudden triumph over Japan, but by a means so astounding and ghastly that even with our celebrations of victory were commingled dark forebodings of world doom.

And now, strained by the uncertainties of a precarious peace, nauseated by gruesome revelations in our war courts of unregenerated man's desperate depravity, distraught by mutual distrust and outbreaking violence between nations, races and classes, men's hearts indeed fail them for fear.

Are the events and conditions of this critical day such as should concern the evangelical forces of America and the world? Is our strategy in any way to be implemented by an understanding of the contemporary scene? Or should evangelicals ignore this present evil age, comforting ourselves that we do our duty alone in witnessing to the reality of another and a spiritual order?

We venture to declare that evangelicals have a responsibility "to serve the present age" in a genuinely prophetic ministry.

In the early days of the Church the Apostle Paul exhorted his son in the gospel in these earnest words: "O Timothy, keep that which is committed to thy trust" (I Timothy 6:20).

In another letter, Paul detailed to Timothy the evils which would threaten this trust, his heritage of piety and sound doctrine. Of the threat which should come to piety, we read from II Timothy, chapter 3: "This know also, that in the last days perilous times shall come. For men shall be lovers of their own selves, covetous, boasters, proud, blasphemers, disobedient to parents, unthankful, unholy, without natural affection, truce-breakers, false accusers, incontinent, . . . lovers of pleasures more than lovers of God."

The threat to sound doctrine Paul predicts in chapter 4: "For the time will come when they will not endure sound doctrine; but after their own lusts shall they heap to themselves teachers, having itching ears; and they shall turn away their ears from the truth, and shall be turned unto fables."

How near, think you, is the fulfillment of Paul's prophecy of these threats to our heritage of piety and faith? Can any deny that the perilous times of which Paul wrote are here?

To carry out Paul's charge to guard the truths

entrusted to us, the National Association of Evangelicals was formed three years ago.

THE SURRENDER TO PAGANISM

We note first today's surrender to paganism in the field of piety and morals. To have called this a pagan age and America a pagan nation a decade ago would have brought to such an assembly as this a shock of surprise if not resentment. Today the charge of paganism is commonplace.

THE PREVALENCE OF SIN

A pagan age is a sinful age. Who will deny the exceeding sinfulness of this age? J. Edgar Hoover some years ago declared that crime had so increased in America that we were virtually in a state of civil war with a criminal army of 4,300,000 active enemies engaged "in a predaceous warfare against society." According to his report this year, that army has now grown to 6,000,000 — an army, he says, which is "larger even than that which did the actual fighting against the Germans and the Japanese." Well has someone said that America has a "perennial carnival of crime!"

Sin has increased in America to a whirlwind chaos of plunder, violence, carnage, lust, and moral anarchy.

THE FADING SENSE OF SIN

But such prevalence of sin does not alone constitute paganism. No doubt at times and places on the frontiers of America our fathers sinned to the same or even greater excess than has this generation, but with this difference: They sinned with a keen consciousness of guilt and knew the smart of outraged ideals; whereas this generation sins without scruple. So long as the sense of sin is acute and ideals remain to rebuke the sinner, paganism is stayed. But sin's prevalence sooner or later succeeds in drugging conscience and corrupting ideals. Then paganism prevails.

Multitudes today have accepted sin without struggle or resistance, because they have lost their ideals. Their sin in Shakespeare's phrasing is "not accidental, but a trade." Their practice accords with a statement in Oscar Wilde's *Picture of Dorian Gray,* "The only way to get rid of a temptation is to yield to it."

Influential leaders of our day have directly contributed to the swelling paganism which is now engulfing society. Dora Russell, onetime wife of Bertrand Russell, in her book, *The Right to Be Happy,* advocates release from our basic sex morality. To secure this release she says, "The idea of sin must be banished."

The late Dr. Freud, high priest of the cult of expressionism, wrote frankly that when his patients, because of his treatment, compromised in sexual conduct, his conscience was clear whatever the outcome.

The most influential man in America in our generation told an audience of youth in 1926: "I confess to pride in this coming generation. You are working out your own salvation ... you play with fire openly where we did in secret, and few of you are burned."

90

With such influences at work upon our youth, we need not marvel that the age of criminals in America has dropped from an average of thirty-five years in 1900 to nineteen in 1945. Since 1939, boys arrested under eighteen have increased in number per year thirty-nine per cent for robbery, forty-eight per cent for murder, and seventy per cent for rape.

A PAGAN GENERATION

Yes, our age is pagan, pagan in the appalling prevalence of sin, but even more pagan in its fading consciousness of guilt for sin. What George Eliot wrote of a villain in fiction too truly describes our generation. She said of Tito in *Romola* that he had "lips that lie with a dimpled smile, eyes with a gleam that no infamy dulls, a conscience that rises from lust and murder without a haggard look."

THE SURRENDER OF FAITH

What power has been sufficient to abolish so completely for society at large our Christian standard of morality?

The power which, as vitriol, has corroded our morals and paganized America is the power of an evil doctrine. That doctrine is naturalism which declares the essential rightness of human nature and the irrelevance of God. It teaches that man needs no Saviour and the universe needs no God. From this reprobate doctrine flows the exceeding sinfulness described in the previous section, for as a man "thinketh in his heart, so is he."

THE PROGRESS OF NATURALISM

In 1859 appeared Darwin's *Origin of Species*. In 1871 — just seventy-five years ago — came his *Descent of Man*. During the years between were published other books advocating naturalism by such men as Huxley and Spencer. The decade of the sixties thus roughly marks the birth of modern naturalism.

Through the remainder of the nineteenth century, naturalism rapidly grew in influence. Already in 1895, Lord Balfour had forebodings of naturalism's later dominance and predicted that when that dominance should come about, naturalism would "eat all nobility out of our conception of conduct and all worth out of our conception of life."

The next year Professor Curtis reported that the root peculiarity of the moral situation was then "a failing sense of personal responsibility for character" and the root peculiarity of the Christian situation "a failing sense of sin." Thus the teaching of naturalism had produced in a single generation a discernible effect upon character and faith.

PROPHETS WITHOUT VISION

The devastation of naturalism has engulfed even the church, polluting the stream of religious teaching and worship. The prophets of this age, as of Jeremiah's, "find no vision from the Lord." They have heeded the "oppositions of science falsely so called," against which Paul warned Timothy, rather than following "the holy scriptures, which are able to make thee wise unto salvation."

How tragic it is that those who should be

prophets of God, getting their vision from the Lord, have chosen instead the dubious dogmas of changing science as the standard of truth by which to judge God's Word.

Such a false prophet was the university pastor of my graduate days. He tried to lead a group of us older students over the modern approach to the Bible, interpreting it, not as the very word of God to man, but as man's word about God. . . .

This false prophet also presented to us Jesus, not as the only begotten Son of God, unique in His divinity, but as the most Godlike man that has ever lived; not as God's downward reach to sinful man, but as man's highest reach toward God. Again I asked a question: "From your evolutionary point of view which maintains the inevitable advance of man to new heights, must we not expect some day a man to arise who will reach higher toward God than did Jesus whom we call Christ? Must we not expect a greater than Christ?" To this question his reply was not so confident, but true to his false premise of naturalism he managed to stammer this answer: "We must be courageous; we must accept the theoretical possibility if not the actuality that a greater than Christ will come!"

TEACHERS THAT TRANSGRESS

But such folly on the part of a preacher not long out of seminary is not so strange when we recall the mishandling of Scripture and the humanizing of Jesus in our leading institutions of theological education. God declared through Isaiah that the teachers of the people had transgressed or wrongly interpreted the truth. And so it is in this age — teachers transgress. For example, Shirley Jackson Case, of the University of Chicago Divinity School, once declared that Jesus held opinions and maintained attitudes not acceptable in our day and our modern problems will not be solved by "imitating an ancient pattern." And A. Bruce Curry, of Union Theological Seminary, has said that the Christian is under no obligation "to align his faith with Jesus or anyone else," but will "develop his religion from many sources," making "full place for truth; some place for Jesus." That the modern view makes religion depend upon man's opinion rather than God's revealed truth has been expressed by Dr. Wieman, of the University of Chicago, in his claim that "Religion is devotion to what one holds to be supremely worthful not only for himelf but for all human beings." Religion, then, is man's idea!

EDUCATION PROGRESSIVELY PAGAN

The blight of naturalism has spread downward from seminary, university, and college to high school, public school, and church school. The trend of modern education makes the child and his immediate desires the center of the universe. We cite examples of the doctrine of naturalism operating in the educational field.

It once fell to my lot, as a conservative member of a discussion panel in an educational conference, to defend the educational and social worth of enduring and time-tested ideals against the radical claim of a state educational officer that the teacher has no right to instruct even young children in what to

94

believe regarding social and moral issues. The teacher's function, he declared, is only to present facts without bias, from which facts even ten-year-olds may reach their own conclusions through group discussion.

University inspectors have reported that in a single day's visitation of a modern high school they witnessed two national heroes dragged through the mud of realistic interpretation in a history class, heard the doctrines of Freud promulgated in a psychology class where repression was rated as mortal sin, and in the assembly listened as the speaker of the day told hundreds of teen-age youth that they behaved like human beings because they were nine-tenths brute. Throughout the day these inspectors observed nothing idealistic or ennobling in that school.

In a distinguished university, a professor has advised his class of prospective high school teachers that without sex experience one is not qualified to teach modern youth. "Experience centered" education here reaches its sordid climax.

These instances, admittedly extreme, nevertheless indicate the direction of powerful currents in modern education which seek to swerve youth from the charted channel of Christian virtues into the whirlpool of paganism.

NATURALISM IN RELIGIOUS EDUCATION

But naturalism has influenced not alone public education and the day school. Much of modern religious education is built upon the sandy foundation of humanistic religion, pragmatic philosophy, and naturalistic ethics.

Convincing evidence of this claim appears annually in the convention programs of that organization which claims to represent the best theory and practice of the day in religious education. In such a program dealing with the religious instruction of early childhood, it was related that a little child ran up to a western window which framed a beautiful sunset, and exclaimed: "O Mother! Who painted that picture?" The mother answered, "I do not know." I could only gather from the response of the leader of the group, a famed specialist in religious education, that it was his judgment that the mother answered wisely and would have erred to take advantage of the child's rapture to press upon her an adult view of God's revelation of himself in His creation.

A young woman of this same group, who had been a teacher in a modern so-called progressive preschool and was then engaged in teaching preschool children in the Sunday school, expressed her surprise and perplexity that she had found no difference between progressive education in the secular school and religious education in the church school.

The Church's surrender of faith has clearly been most disastrously achieved from within the Church through the subtle influence of naturalistic teachings which have permeated the Church's educational program from seminary downward to the cradle.

CORRUPT MINDS

We have reviewed the evidence of surrender both

of piety and doctrine in this modern age. This surrender we have connected with the growing dominance of naturalism in thought and life. We turn now to search the secret of naturalism's grip on men's minds, to note its peril in this atomic era, and to mark its final despair.

THE LOGIC OF DESIRE

Why has naturalism made such rapid conquest of modern civilization? Is its factual evidence so plentiful and its logic so compelling that no other doctrine is tenable? No, for the logic of naturalism is the logic of desire, not the logic of truth.

Men eagerly accept naturalism because they wish to escape the condemnation of sin and the humbling sense of dependence upon God. As Dr. Zwemer has said, "Skeptics and agnostics cannot leave Christianity alone because Christianity will not leave them alone."

It is on this basis of willful unbelief that Paul interprets the apostasy reported in II Timothy 3: "These also resist the truth: men of corrupt minds, reprobate concerning the faith."

Elsewhere (II Thessalonians 2), Paul tells of those who perish "because they received not the love of the truth, that they might be saved." Those of whom Paul here writes did not love the truth. The error which damned them was not the error of ignorance but of their ultimate preference: they desired that a lie be true! Their unbelief is explained, not by lack of sufficient facts to bring conviction of truth, but by desire's distortion of the truth and their pleasure in unrighteousness.

Scripture thus clearly teaches that belief is a moral as well as an intellectual act of human personality.

REASON, THE SERVANT OF DESIRE

As belief has yielded largely to the domination of desire, so reason likewise has surrendered its throne.

Until a quarter-century ago, human engineers generally assumed the validity of that ancient dictum of Socrates, "Knowledge is virtue." According to such a philosophy, education for character is indeed simple. Teach the child the rules of morals, and you guarantee his obeying them, even against the downward pull of instinctive desires.

Now we know better. Men of keen minds but wicked hearts will cunningly devise evil. With the development of modern paganism the intellect of man has become a mere instrument for attaining the ends of impulse, appetite, and passion. No longer master, reason is the servant of desire and, as phrased by one of our moderns, has no more claim to dignity as a means for discovering truth than has a pig's snout!

KNOWLEDGE IS POWER!

No, knowledge is not virtue, but it is power. The greater the knowledge, the greater the power for evil if the heart is wicked. H. G. Wells once characterized history as a race between education and catastrophe, but he spoke a dangerous half-truth. Education itself if of the wrong kind brings greater disaster than does ignorance. One has truly said that to educate reason without changing desire is to place high-powered guns in the hands of savages. And now savages may tamper with the basic energy of the universe. Hence that pall of fear which hangs over all the civilized world. Will the power of the atom be directed to human welfare or to the destruction of civilization?

History offers little encouragement, for essentially every advance in man's power has seemed to increase his wickedness. The danger is frightfully clear that, with the decline of ethics and religious controls, we all are now subject to the disintegrating heat of primal forces which at any time may be let loose by the diabolic cunning of sophisticated savages.

NATURALISM'S DESPAIR

A half-century of naturalism has brought us to that nadir foreseen by Lord Balfour — conduct has lost all nobility and human life all worth.

Someone has pointed out that Thomas Huxley, persuasive advocate of naturalism in the nineteenth century, tried to dismiss God from His universe while attempting to retain a place therein of moral worth and dignity for man. Now his grandson, Aldous Huxley, member of the literary cult of disillusioned moderns, can find nothing noble, dignified, or worthy in man. It is not possible for man to surrender belief in God and long retain belief in himself.

Strange paradox! From naturalism's teaching of man's sufficiency, we now reap the harvest of human futility and frustration. The high drama of human history has shriveled, as one phrases it, to "a brief and transitory episode in the life of one of the meanest of the planets.'' Man is described as ''an ape that chatters to itself glibly of kinship with archangels while filthily it digs for groundnuts.'' Another says that man ''has no reason to suppose his own life has any more meaning than the life of the humblest insect that crawls from one annihilation to another.''

Even more sobering than such literary pessimism is the philosopher's portrayal of human futility in an age of unleashed power. Bertrand Russell says, '' . . . the fairest achievements of man are destined to be destroyed at last by the trampling march of unconscious power,'' and the best a man can do is ''hold an unyielding despair.'' Again he says, ''Brief and powerless is man's life. On him and all his race the slow sure doom falls pitiless and dark. Blind to good and evil, reckless of destruction, omnipotent matter rolls on its relentless way.''

And thus the dirge continues in a rising wail, for the nineteenth century's surrender of God has brought the twentieth century to despair of man.

"TO SERVE THE PRESENT AGE"

What course should evangelicals take in a world so fully surrendered to paganism and apostasy?

INDIFFERENCE? OR DESPAIR?

Some evangelicals are inclined to retreat before the enemy, withdrawing within themselves as a defense against the world's corruption. We read in history of those eras when the pious, ignoring a lost world, have sought the isolation of the desert or the wilderness monastery; or perhaps in communal bands have colonized secluded and fertile valleys, there seeking to protect their piety in sterile aloofness from worldly and secular institutions and customs. This is the route of indifference to a pagan world.

But other professed evangelicals remain in a pagan world and may even partake of the world's paganism. They have no hope of revival nor of improvement in world conditions through processes of revival. In the words of a representative of this group, God's purpose is being fulfilled "in the destruction of democracy and decency and the trend toward Antichrist" and in civilization's total collapse. This is the way of despair.

SOOTHING COMPROMISE?

Few evangelicals would agree with the pompous layman who asked a group of ministers what their ideas were of the purpose of a sermon. One preacher ventured to suggest that the sermon should instruct. But the layman said, "No! For what right has the preacher to set his ideas of truth against another's beliefs?" Then I had the temerity to declare that a sermon should disturb. Wrong again! For what right has the preacher to tell others their sins?

The layman then answered his own query: "The purpose of a sermon," he said, "is to soothe."

PREACH THE WORD!

But the fully Christian course is neither indifference to a pagan world nor despair; nor yet to soothe it in its impious apostasy. Let's turn to the record of Paul's charge to Timothy. There we should find light for our path. Here it is: "I charge thee therefore before God, and the Lord Jesus Christ, who shall judge the quick and the dead at his appearing and his kingdom; preach the word; be instant in season, out of season; reprove, rebuke, exhort with all longsuffering and doctrine. . . . But watch thou in all things, endure afflictions, do the work of an evangelist, make full proof of thy ministry."

Careful search of this passage gives no encouragement to indifference, to despair, nor to soothing compromise. But there is no escaping Paul's command so to preach the Word as both to instruct and to disturb! He prefaces his charge to Timothy with this statement of the ground thereof:

"All scripture is given by inspiration of God, and is profitable for doctrine, for reproof, for correction, for instruction in righteousness: that the man of God may be perfect, throughly furnished unto all good works."

PROFITABLE FOR DOCTRINE

Evangelicals must revive doctrinal preaching and support the same by thorough scholarship. Men of science have consecrated their intellects to the task of solving the mystery of the atom and have succeeded in unlocking the basic energy of the universe. Evangelicals cannot be conscience-clear if, to the task of releasing the spiritual treasures of wisdom and knowledge which are hid in Christ, they summon a consecration less complete than the consecration of scientists to the task of releasing the destructive forces of the material order. In the age we now enter, the mediocre in faith, in thought, and in practical endeavor is foredoomed to futility.

In the face of world crisis, to abandon mental and moral and spiritual preparation for frenzied exhortation in a despairing urgency to glean a sheaf here and there before the impending doom falls will but short-circuit our efforts and prevent our entering the great harvest fields which now are opening.

I am in hearty accord with those who believe the evangelical movement needs in this day a renewed scholarship and a revitalized apologetic. The National Association of Evangelicals has intellectual resources to meet the challenge of this need, and without sacrifice of evangelistic fervor must bear this responsibility. This is a pressing task for the decade we face.

PROFITABLE FOR REPROOF

But a strengthened apologetic is not the only need if evangelicals are more effectively to promote the extension of the gospel. We have earlier pointed to scriptural proof that both apostasy and paganism primarily spring from evil desire expressed in willful unbelief and pleasure in unrighteousness.

Hence, logic and apologetics alone cannot meet and overthrow the arch-forces of apostasy and paganism. A sound apologetic is of great importance in stabilizing the entire structure of Christian faith, confirming individual believers therein, helping the honest doubter to a firm footing, and leaving the dishonest apostate without excuse. But the strongest apologetic will be turned aside by a perverted heart. Argument engages the intellectual powers of both sides in exciting skirmishes on the field of battle but leaves safely entrenched the cherished lie of the inmost soul.

Evangelical strategy must go beyond direct frontal assault upon the outer intellectual defenses of apostasy, and include a moral flank attack which by-passes the rational front of unbelief to search out and probe the undercover depths of perverted desire. I am persuaded that our evangelism must more and more follow the moral-shock method employed by our Lord on sinners at both cultural extremes, the Samaritan woman at the lower and Nicodemus at the upper level.

In fact, there is growing evidence that the moral impact of the gospel is effective with untutored heathen as we have hitherto failed to realize because of our commitment to a prolonged program of Christian culture which we have thought necessary to evangelism — and which too often has become a substitute for evangelism.

Experience with youth on the non-Christian campus has likewise confirmed my belief that the most effective gospel approach to the young intellectuals of this age is not the reasoned apologetic so common in my student generation — and which so often ended in compromise of Christian faith — but is rather the moral-shock approach characterized by confrontation, encounter, challenge, moral crisis, choice, and personal commitment. Why? Because doubt is more often moral in basis than intellectual.

The moral-shock method in gospel preaching is nothing new. Frontier preachers a century ago were skilled in its use, and those most evangelistically successful today employ it. Its essence is proclaiming rather than defending the Word of God which carries its own conviction.

> For the word of God is quick, and powerful, and sharper than any twoedged sword, piercing even to the dividing asunder of soul and spirit, and of the joints and marrow, and is a discerner of the thoughts and intents of the heart.
> *Hebrews 4:12*

THE EVANGELICAL TRIAD

To clarify the evangelical mission in a pagan world we outline three major aspects of evangelical Christianity, each with its distinctive function. All three are so important that none can safely be neglected or sacrificed to the dominance of another. These are:

Piety, the pattern of Christian living,

Orthodoxy, the pattern of Christian thinking,

Power, the heart-dynamic of Christian experience.

An emphasis on piety to the neglect of doctrine too often leads to the wrecking of orthodoxy — and eventually piety itself collapses.

A pietistic group has come to my attention which throughout the years until recently maintained a policy of strict isolation to protect its piety. Of late, however, this group has veered sharply toward doctrinal liberalism. One of its older leaders has confessed that many of its younger preachers now deny the deity of Christ.

Another minority group of strongly pietistic emphasis has exerted a powerful influence for good upon the religious life of English-speaking peoples but has minimized the importance of doctrine. This

105

movement in theological complexion of its lesser bodies today ranges all the way from rankest Unitarianism to evangelical orthodoxy.

Piety alone is no sufficient guarantee of orthodoxy.

On the other hand, a strong and strident orthodoxy may be linked with worldliness and sin. Not long ago a true evangelical serving a rigidly orthodox group exclaimed to me, "My people are so orthodox — but so worldly!" Dr. Ockenga, in *Our Evangelical Faith,* trenchantly points out this weakness of much of today's orthodoxy. He says: "The great criticism of fundamentalism is that Christianity is limited too much to the historical, objective, dogmatic truth without a carry over into life. . . . Dead orthodoxy can be as great a reproach to Christianity as is unbelief."

Orthodoxy then is no sufficient guarantee of piety, and evangelical Christianity cannot meet a pagan world in the strength of cold orthodoxy alone.

Nor is emphasis upon power alone sufficient. Unrestrained by piety and undirected by sound doctrine, power may run amuck in fantastic heresies, fanatical extravagance of emotion, or appalling derelictions in conduct. Not long ago I sought for hours in vain to uproot the heresy into which a former friend of mine had fallen through exaggerated emphasis upon experience with corresponding neglect of the Word.

FORMS OF GODLINESS PLUS POWER

True evangelicalism maintains the balance of high moral idealism and reasoned doctrine, the symmetry of clearly patterned piety and orthodoxy. Orthodoxy and piety are the essential forms or directing restraints of religion, serving as banks to a stream. Without these forms, religion flattens out and stagnates, just as a river without banks becomes a marsh. Such is religious liberalism — a river without banks. Evangelicals must keep both banks clearly defined if the channel is to be kept open.

But true evangelicalism demands more than orthodoxy and piety. We may maintain a legalistic piety and a rigidly formal orthodoxy and have no current and therefore no power. Yes, it is possible to maintain at least for a time these forms of godliness, orthodoxy, and piety while denying the power of godliness which, according to our statement of evangelical faith, is the Holy Spirit. We are then a channel without a stream, as the Grand Coulee and the Dry Falls of northeastern Washington through and over which once rushed the mighty Columbia but which ages ago were deserted by the river to stand there through millenniums in their solemn majesty and awful emptiness, mute reminders of a departed power and glory.

CONCLUSION

The National Association of Evangelicals from its beginnings in the Saint Louis Conference has again and again experienced the outpourings of the Holy Spirit upon national gatherings and more local assemblies. We will "serve the present age, our calling to fulfill" as we maintain a firm orthodoxy and an unsullied piety as the channel through which surges that power of the Holy Spirit which alone is greater than the power of sin and unbelief in a pagan and apostate world.

With that power, we seek not safety for ourselves in withdrawal from the world and indifference to its needs; nor in the midst of a pagan order do we despair of the effectiveness of the gospel which still is "the power of God through faith unto salvation," for with that power of the Holy Spirit, greater is He that is in us than he that is in the world!

*Essentially as given
at Asbury Theological Seminary,
November 21, 1951*

God and the Nations

Behold, I am the Lord, the God of all flesh: is there anything too hard for me?   Jeremiah 32:27

I bring you this morning, not a travelogue, but simply my observations on conditions in the nations in Europe I visited, and my reactions thereto in the framework of Scripture.

———

The world is at its extremity, seemingly a hopeless extremity. We have international strife; there is corruption in the body-politic; personal morality drags in the gutter; confusion if not treachery is exhibited by world leaders. The ominous rhythm of marching hosts is the insistent undertone of daily events. The fires of Moloch glow red for the sacrifice of the world's finest youth. Men's hearts are failing them for fear, and even Christians despair of the noble experiment called civilization.

The world's sinsickness seems past remedy. The world is done! Burned out at the center by the raging fire of sin, and soon to be burnt up by the judgment of an angry God. Can God prevail against the sweeping tides of sin without utterly destroying the earth in cataclysmic judgment?

THE BLIGHT OF SIN

I have seen the blight of sin on the nations of Europe. I have seen the destruction that an unholy war has wrought on great cities such as London — a destruction that swept homes as well as munitions factories, that snuffed out the lives of babes and helpless children along with criminals, that wrecked churches along with brothels.

And I have seen the wreckage of Berlin, so vast that decades and generations will be required to remove the rubble and rebuild; and scars will remain the duration of time. Great areas of Berlin have been pounded to powder. Proud monuments that once vaunted German conquests have been laid low. This great city, built upon sandy, marshy flats is to have its mountain, built of non-salvable rubble. The vast base of that mountain has already been laid and trucks carry the city's debris up a serpentine road to the mountain's growing summit. Yes, Berlin is building a mountain of its ruins, a costly monument to sin's madness.

I have seen Dachau, utterly depressing, where multiplied thousands of Hitler's victims died by horrible violence. I have seen Dachau's death chamber, its gas chamber, its crematory furnaces, the place of execution by pistol fire, the base of the old gallows, and the "hanging tree" now itself dead — a stark, somber ghost. I have read the Dachau motto over the door, "Never again!" But I cannot escape the haunting lesson that Dachau teaches concerning the corruption of unregenerate human nature, nor its warning that wickedness "on the loose" is capable of future multiplied Dachaus.

Drop down the map of Europe to Rome. In the suburbs of this ancient city I have seen the cave to which hundreds of Rome's residents disappeared mysteriously from the city's streets during World War II, their mangled and decomposed bodies later to be discovered where Hitler's machine guns had poured a stream of lead into the cavern's mass of humanity in wholesale murder.

And near this modern cave of horrors I have groped my way along the subterranean galleries of the catacombs where early Christians gathered in the presence of thousands of their dead to worship God in secret with a measure of uncertain safety.

I have looked across the Circus Maximus to the Palace of the Caesars on the Palatine Hill. From the balconies of that Palace, royalty cheered as Christians in the circus below were torn apart by the lions.

Below the Palace of the Caesars on the opposite side of the Palatine Hill I have seen the ruins of the Roman Forum with its remnants of the Basilica Julian where the Apostle Paul was tried and condemned to death. And I have followed portions of the course by which Paul was led from the city through a gate now named in his honor; and outside the city walls I have looked upon the spot where his head rolled from his body as his neck was cleft asunder by the executioner's ax.

The evidences of brutality, of bestiality, of lust and violence are many in this sin-fevered world.

GOD'S JUDGMENT UPON SIN

There are evidences also of God's judgment upon

sin. The glory that was Rome has faded. The empire of the Caesars has been brought to judgment in history, and the Caesars themselves now suffer the judgments of eternity. Mussolini, who would be successor to the Caesars, has been judged, and the balcony from which he loved to address Italy in the presence of the great monuments of history is today just another balcony, silent and ordinary.

Distant rumblings of judgment against the Church that has so betrayed the tender and compassionate Christ, and has perverted the simple faith of Rome's early martyrs, can now be heard before that judgment strikes in fury. Humanly, there is no hope for Italy's oppressed masses, and revolution can be averted only by a reforming revival of religion.

God's judgment was visited upon the wicked city of Pompeii nearly nineteen centuries ago. This ancient city of great wealth and culture was overtaken at the height of its prosperity by a strange doom which preserved it for exploration in our day. I have walked the streets of this excavated city, and have viewed its baths, and have seen its temple ruins, and have looked through its houses. The elaborateness of domestic arrangements, the magnificence and elegance of the city's dwellings, and the advanced development even of its plumbing amaze and humble the modern traveler.

But coupled with luxury and advanced civilization in Pompeii was a moral corruption, the evidence of which was sealed by the city's doom to be opened in modern times — such evidence of corruption that guides may not disclose it to mixed groups even in this sophisticated age, Yes, judgment for its vileness came upon Pompeii, even as upon Sodom in the days of Lot.

Modern history speaks of judgment as well. In those long years of the early forties the judgment of Hitler seemed to tarry, but now in the sweeping perspective of history, how brief was Hitler's day of dominance. Near the Austrian border in southeastern Bavaria, I was taken by Chaplain Hayes and military car up a lovely mountainside of the Bavarian Alps — lovely until we reached a scene of weird desolation and destruction. We came first upon a great hotel in ruins; this had been Hitler's mountain guesthouse. Above these ruins we saw the shattered barracks of Hitler's proud storm troopers. Then we drove to the back yard of Hermann Goering's once-lovely mountain home, now desolate in stark ruins. Nearby we explored the massive wreckage of Hitler's palatial villa.

A few days later in Berlin, three or four hundred miles to the north, I looked from an American army bus in the communist sector upon the site of the Chancellery and saw, lifted above the debris, the concrete bunkers Hitler had built for his last-ditch safety and that of his intimates. Here Hitler met his death. He has been judged in history; he is being judged in eternity!

But there is the irony of Paris; proud Paris; gay Paris; wicked Paris; seemingly untouched by war and maintaining yet her beauty. There sin, unblushing, walks abroad. Why a wrecked London, a ruined Liverpool, a blasted Naples, a shattered Munich, a pulverized Berlin, when sinful Paris swaggers still in impudent freedom from judgment!

When I recall Paris, I share the psalmist's complaint against the wicked whom he saw "in great power and spreading himself like a green bay tree." But judgment, although delayed, is certain, and one day the psalmist's further words concerning the wicked will be applied to Paris: "Yet he passed away, and, lo, he was not: the end of the wicked shall be cut off."

In the face of all the evil of the world, can God establish righteousness? Can He save our civilization from destruction and mankind from collapse into savagery?

THE LESSON FROM JEREMIAH

More and more I am convinced that we find answers to the world's great problems in the revealed Word, not by blind chance which opens the Bible to particular passages to be taken out of their context and literally applied, but by intelligent and reverent study of the Word to discover and apply its great underlying truths, its sweeping compelling convictions.

On my homeward voyage I was forcibly struck by a passage from Jeremiah, and as later I reflected thereon, my European experiences assumed the perspective I now attempt to convey to others.

In Jeremiah's day, affairs in Judah were in an exceedingly sad state. Following a period of reform under the good king, Josiah, the nation quickly and completely backslid into idolatry and rebellion against the law. Josiah's reforms had not been spiritual revival; he had imposed and enforced

114

outward righteousness upon a people whose hearts had not been changed, and after his death the reaction was extreme.

By nature Jeremiah was timid and retiring, but the call of God was upon him, and with unswerving loyalty he carried out God's commission, "Thou shalt go to all that I shall send thee, and whatever I command thee thou shalt speak" (Jeremiah 1:7). Jeremiah's devotion to God and God's people led him to say hard things, declaring the judgments of God against sin and rebellion. For this he was rejected by his nation, his village, his family. Having prophesied that Jerusalem would fall under the siege that had been laid against it by the Chaldeans, Jeremiah was imprisoned for alleged treason.

Under such circumstances God instructed him to purchase a piece of land in his family village of Anathoth near Jerusalem. Ever obedient, Jeremiah complied, notwithstanding the impending fall of the city following which, no doubt, property would be confiscated by the conquerors and the inhabitants of the city would be carried away captive.

The record as given in Jeremiah 32 tells how Jeremiah bought the land from a kinsman, weighed out to him the silver, and executed ''the evidence of the purchase'' in duplicate before witnesses. He then instructed Baruch, his scribe, to deposit these documents in an earthen vessel for preservation according to the practice of those times.

> For thus saith the Lord of hosts, the God of Israel; Houses and fields and vineyards shall be possessed again in this land.
> (v. 15)

What a meaningless transaction: a prisoner for treason, buying land in a doomed city with all the legal technicalities and formalities that would be proper if Judah and Jerusalem were to stand forever! It seems that after the transaction Jeremiah himself was tested in his faith and went to the Lord in prayer. His opening declaration, even by its strong assertion, suggests the temptation to doubt that assailed him. He exercised his "will to believe," as did the man who once said to Jesus, "Lord, I believe: help thou mine unbelief." Here are Jeremiah's words:

> Ah, Lord God! behold, thou hast made the heaven and the earth by thy great power and stretched out arm, and there is nothing too hard for thee.   (v. 17)

The prophet proceeded to review the case of God's gracious dealings with Judah, Judah's miserable backsliding, and the judgment that was about to fall upon Jerusalem. He concludes:

> And thou hast said unto me, O Lord God, Buy thee the field for money, and take witnesses; for [whereas] the city is given into the hand of the Chaldeans.   (v. 25)

And God answered in the words that prefaced our opening and which we now repeat:

> Behold, I am the Lord, the God of all flesh: is there anything too hard for me?   (v. 27)

Then the Lord reviewed the backslidings of Judah, but added:

> Men shall buy fields for money, and subscribe evidences, and seal them, and take witnesses in the land of Benjamin, and in the places about Jerusalem, and in the cities of Judah and in the cities of the mountains, and in the cities of the valley, and in the cities of the south; for I will cause their captivity to return, saith the Lord.
>
> (v. 44)

> ... Again there shall be heard in this place which ye say shall be desolate without man and without beast, even in the cities of Judah, and in the streets of Jerusalem ... the voice of joy, and the voice of gladness, the voice of the bridegroom and the voice of the bride, the voice of them that shall say, Praise the Lord of hosts: for the Lord is good; for his mercy endureth for ever. . . .   (33:10-11)

Thus Jeremiah preached and prophesied not only God's judgments, but likewise His love and mercy. From the sad aftermath of Josiah's reforms, Jeremiah well knew the futility of moral reform without spiritual rebirth, and through him God already had declared the New Covenant:

> I will put my law in their inward parts, and write it in their hearts; and will be their God, and they shall be my people.   (31:33)

Jeremiah's obedience in purchasing the field under the very shadow of judgment on Judah's violation of the Old Covenant was a dramatic assertion of his faith in the New Covenant. God has never abrogated the New Covenant, but rather has reaffirmed it in the record of the New Testament again and again.

GOD CAN!

Men once claimed the support of Scripture for a

doctrine of personal determinism according to which many were elected to damnation. Reaction followed this harsh doctrine, giving dominance to a doctrine of inevitable progress consummating in a millennium of righteousness. But under this delusion of beneficent determinism the social order rapidly descended into paganism until explosive eruptions of savagery dispelled this blind faith in inevitable progress.

Let us not stumble into yet a third fatalistic error toward which the prevailing mood of theological reaction tends. I refer to that dispensational determinism which paralyzes Christian faith by its despair of the gospel's power in our age to meet human need through spiritual revival and social reform born of revival, and which admits no alternative to early destruction of the present world-order by God's inexorable judgment against sin.

God is not yet done with man on this earth if only man will accept God's claim upon him. Let it again be said — God has not abrogated the New Covenant. He awaits man's response to proffered mercy that He may validate that covenant in this desperate day. God's judgments do no violence to His mercy, for those judgments may be averted by man's repentance, even as the promises of God are contingent upon man's obedience. If we but listen, we shall hear with Jeremiah the Lord's promise, "I will cause their captivity to return," and "Again there shall be heard ... the voice of joy, and the voice of gladness ... the voice of them that shall say, Praise the Lord of hosts: for the Lord is good; for his mercy endureth for ever. . . ."

Christians have no business closing shop and yielding to the paralysis of despair because sin abounds, for where sin abounds there may grace much more abound. Rather than submerging me in pessimism, my experiences and observations in Europe have challenged my faith, and my courage was inspired by tokens of God's grace bestowed even in the midst of wretchedness and sin.

In Germany, Pastor Scholz is [1951] carrying on a great work even in the Russian Zone where he superintends Methodist churches. During the war he was bombed out of his church and home in the heart of Berlin, but from the rubble and ruin of the former church has arisen a greater church as the center of German Methodism.

In Berlin also I visited Bible institutes or seminars which train young women for child evangelism. Many of the students are war orphans from the Russian Zone who courageously return to their own people to serve in kindergartens, recreation centers and in home evangelism.

I have expressed my perplexity that Paris seemingly has escaped judgment. Is it because of the "ten righteous"? For in Paris I found the "City of Refuge" — a great Salvation Army center where the gospel of redemption is preached. There I heard radiant testimonies and a gospel message under which seekers knelt in an old-fashioned penitent form. This in wicked Paris!

In poor, priest-ridden Italy, under the shadow of Vesuvius and near the beautiful Bay of Naples, I was guest in a one-time fashionable villa where now a school is conducted for former priests and seminarians of Catholicism who are seeking to become Protestant preachers. And I have preached to an eager and responsive mission audience gathered from a wretched boat-building suburb of Naples where courageous workers challenge the Church of Rome with the gospel.

In Methodism's Central Hall, London, I attended sessions of the city-wide evangelistic campaign, organized to give a spiritual emphasis to the Festival of Britain. There I heard searching gospel messages, one of them by the Anglican Bishop of Barking.

The program of the World Conference of Methodism in Oxford commemorated in large measure the man whose heart-warming thawed England from the icy chill of the religious formalism of the eighteenth century, and sparked a revival to produce radical moral and social reforms that swung the entire course of English history from its former road to revolution. A high point of the Oxford conference was the sermon by Dr. Sangster which held spellbound a crowded house as he gave in clear outline the essentials of the Methodist message. A second mountain peak was reached in a morning session on evangelism when Professor Pawson brought the most spiritually stirring message of the ten days. In the holy hush that followed the climaxing conclusion, the chairman with great discernment called on the speaker to lead in prayer. And we were lifted to the very throne of God!

I have seen the pulpits, outdoor and indoor, of Wesley and Whitefield; the market-cross and the tomb of Wesley's father at Epworth where John

Wesley preached; City Road Chapel in London and the site of the foundry which preceded it as Methodism's center; the New Room at Bristol; Whitefield's chapel in Bristol and another he built in the Kingswood suburb; the site of the brick-fields in Bristol where John Wesley yielded his high-church prejudices and first preached in the fields; — Oh so many places have I trod where the early saints of Methodism walked and labored and preached and suffered — and proved that God could deliver from evil and corruption in the eighteenth century, and will stay His judgments when men repent!

How then can I doubt that all this will happen again in the twentieth century if God can find yielded human channels and if men will respond with repentance to the offer of grace! As in Paul's day, and again in Wesley's, the gospel in our day is the power of God unto salvation.

*The final official message
given to the Free Methodist Church
at its 1964 General Conference*

The River of Spiritual Life

> There is a river, the streams whereof shall make glad the city of God, the holy place of the tabernacles of the Most High.   Psalm 46:4

THE PARABLE OF THE RIVER

On the occasion of bringing the pastoral address to the General Conference of 1939 I pointed out that orthodoxy and piety are the essential forms or directing restraints of spiritual life, as banks to a stream; that without these forms the spiritual life flattens out and stagnates, even as a river without banks becomes a marsh. These banks of sound doctrine and holy living, I said, must be maintained if there is to be an open channel for the passage of the current. But I warned that we may continue to the end a Quaker piety and a doctrinal fundamentalism, and yet die at the heart from loss of the Spirit; for it is possible to maintain at least for a time the forms of godliness, piety, and orthodoxy, while denying the power of godliness. We should become a channel without a current, as the Grand Coulee and the Dry Falls of northeastern Washington, through and over which once rushed the mighty Columbia but which ages since were deserted by the river to stand in awesome emptiness as mute reminders of a departed power and glory.

This morning, twenty-five years later, I review these words and amplify them to provide a background for quite another message. A concern of my ministry since that pastoral message — and even before — has been to define and to guard the banks of piety on the one hand and those of orthodoxy on the other, lest the stream of spiritual life escape its channel and flatten into impotence. If the bank of orthodoxy (Christian belief) should be inundated at any point, the current will escape its channel to lose itself in the marshy flats of doctrinal liberalism; if the bank of piety (Christian living) should yield to the erosion of compromise, the current will drain off into the treacherous morass of worldliness and settle into stagnation.

The banks of Christian belief and Christian piety, and the channel between them, provide the form of godliness; but a channel and its confining banks are not enough. According to our parable, without the flowing stream between its banks, a channel is but a *coulee,* an abandoned riverbed. If no life of the Spirit courses through the *form* of godliness there can be no *power* of godliness. To yield an effective Christian life and witness, sound doctrine and firm piety must be vitalized by an inner experience born of the Spirit of God. The empty form signifies not merely lack of the power of godliness but the very denial thereof.

The source of the Christian's power of godliness is worship, broadly conceived as the Christian's communion with God by which he receives the power of the Spirit to overcome temptation and to render effective service. This power is not supplied in bulk to be retained in a reservoir as potential energy, but is rather as kinetic energy, constantly supplied according to need in response to worship and the daily prayer of faith. "As thy days, so shall thy strength be." Christian experience, which arises in worship as the human spirit comes into contact with divine power, is not an end in itself nor merely the means to religious emotion and ecstasy. Its true end is service to God and man through stewardship of every good gift God bestows.

From an overview on some high hillside, let us trace the course of this stream of spiritual life. Its source is in those distant mountains of God. The stream is released from its mountain barriers, on God's part by His willingness to give the Holy Spirit to those who ask Him; on man's part by worship in the reading of God's Word, the prayer of faith, the song of praise.

As the stream breaks out of the foothills and flows across the plain, we discern its course, well marked by the fruitful foliage edging its banks — on one side Christian piety, on the other Christian doctrine. It is a stream that submits to the control of its channel. It does not break through its banks to lose itself in the stagnation of desolate swamps, but on its way to the great ocean of eternity it shares its flow with those who ask of God the Holy Spirit, and who open their hearts and lives to receive the cleansing current of divine power.

We see in this parable of the stream of spiritual life five essential features: the restraining bank of doctrine; the opposite bank of piety; between these banks the stream of divine power as the living current of Christian experience; the source of this power in Christian worship; the issue of this power in service to man and glory to God.

THE RIVER'S CENTRAL SOURCE AND ITS OVERFLOWINGS

All five features of the river are important, else I should not have included them in the parable. Our purpose on this occasion is not to place primary emphasis on either the bank of doctrine or the bank of piety, nor yet on service and stewardship as our contribution to the prosperity of God's kingdom. These features may appear at times in our consideration of what are even greater in importance — the character of the stream itself which is the moving current of our being, and those relationships of worship we maintain to keep the channel clear toward God as the source of the stream of our spiritual life. In worship and its effects within Christian experience, that point is reached where the human is consciously aware of the touch of the Divine, and the purity and power of the current itself best insure the progress of all other features of the Christian life. Our message will therefore take us from life's surface to the depths, from the periphery to the center of our being.

The writer of the book of Proverbs points to life's center and its depths in the exhortation, "Keep thy heart with all diligence; for out of it are the issues of life" (Proverbs 4:23). In this and many another passage of Scripture, the term *heart* stands for the very core of man's being, the essential self, the "I" which is the seat of conscience and the source of our moral and spiritual capacity and activity. Terms translated as this word *heart* appear in the English Bible a thousand times, and this concept of a central core of being underlies the entire structure of biblical psychology. Christian devotion involves this core and flows from the inner being of a born-again Christian throughout his life relationships — we may say, through all the issues or overflowings of his life. Again we use the figure of a river, for the word translated "issues" is sometimes rendered "springs," suggesting the source of a stream.

To discover what are the major issues or overflowings of the heart, we turn to Luke 10:27. The lawyer who had sought to ensnare our Lord drew upon his knowledge of the Hebrew Scriptures to answer the question with which he had sought to embarrass Jesus, but by which he himself was to be embarrassed. The incident is not our present concern, but the lawyer's quotation of the ancient Scriptures is: "Thou shalt love the Lord thy God with all thy heart, and with all thy soul, and with all thy strength, and with all thy mind; and thy neighbour as thyself."

The streams that issue or flow from the *heart* are here called "soul," "strength," and "mind." We note briefly each in turn.

Terms translated *soul* appear frequently in the Bible, sometimes with a meaning almost synonymous with *heart,* but generally carrying a connotation that points to the moving, striving, desiring, feeling aspects of our nature. In his *Notes on the New Testament* John Wesley interpreted the words, "with all thy soul," by the phrase, "with the warmest affection." This meaning is conveyed in popular usage today by the adjective *soulful*," the dictionary definition of which is "full of feeling; deeply emotional." We may say, then, that *soul* stands for man's affectional, emotional, and temperamental capacities and characteristics.

Strength represents energy available for action. When the direction of this energy is toward an end having moral significance, we call the resulting conduct good or bad, moral or immoral.

The meaning of *mind* is clear, embracing man's intellectual capacities and processes, in the accepted usage of our own day.

The four significant words we have considered in this passage; namely, heart, soul, strength, and mind, are not all on the same level of meaning or importance. In his footnote to Luke 10:27, Weymouth has pointed out the significant fact that in the Greek the preposition changes from "out of" in connection with "heart," to "in" with the other three — soul, strength, and mind. Thus primacy is accorded the heart as the source of the other three. Weymouth's comment makes this clear. He says:

> *With*] Lit. "out of," the heart standing for the centre of the whole mental life in all its varied range; then the preposition changes to a thrice repeated "in." The love flows out from its central source into three channels, manifesting itself in the several spheres of feeling [soul], will [strength], and intellect [mind].

These following words of Jesus develop this same concept of the heart as that central spring of man's being from which flow all the issues of life: "For out of the heart proceed evil thoughts, murders, adulteries, fornications, thefts, false witness, blasphemies" (Matthew 15:19), ". . . covetousness, wickedness, . . . an evil eye, . . . pride, foolishness . . ." (Mark 7:22).

It requires no psychiatrist or psychologist to discern in this shameful list the pollutions of the soul by foul desires, of the strength by wicked deeds, of the mind by evil thoughts — all are there; the outflowings of an unclean heart. In sharp contrast to such corruptions of human nature, Jesus describes in these brief words the issues of a good man's heart: "A good man out of the good treasure of the heart bringeth forth good things" (Matthew 12:35).

THE ESSENTIAL CHARACTER
OF THE RIVER IS LOVE

We have seen that the First Commandment makes it a man's first duty to love God from his inmost and utmost being, out of that deepest spring of all his energies, the heart; and then to yield every area of his redeemed personality to the outrush of love: all his soul in pure affections and holy desires, his entire strength in righteous conduct and obedient service, his whole mind in pure thoughts and disciplined judgment. If the issues of life are to be holy, their source must be guarded carefully against pollution. "Keep your heart with all vigilance; for from it flow the springs of life" (Proverbs 4:23, RSV).

Further development of Luke 10:27 is found in I Corinthians 13. The preceding chapter has presented an account of Christian gifts and graces, but promises to show a more excellent way than all these. Reading this thirteenth chapter, one discovers that the more excellent way is love, flowing from the central being of that man who is right with God and with his neighbor. In truth, this chapter is an elaboration or development of the terse outline of Luke 10:27. Its units of thought group themselves under the four key words of the outline, so that when sorted according to these terms few of these units remain unclassified. Note this analysis.

SOUL, STANDING FOR THE FEELING OR AFFECTIONAL NATURE

From this chapter's enumeration of the soul's affections or desires, we find no hint that the more excellent way consists either in the ecstasy of the movement or in any sustained mood of pleasure. We find explicitly stated, however, that love does not tolerate pride, envy, selfishness, anger, and the like sinful affections.

STRENGTH, EXPRESSED IN ACTION, CONDUCT, AND SERVICE

In this connection the chapter refers to speaking with the tongues of men and of angels (for speech is behavior, good or bad); to giving all one's goods to feed the poor, and one's body to be burned (good works indeed — even unto martyrdom!); to moving mountains by faith (even the exercise of miraculous spiritual power!). But Paul does not find in action as service, sacrifice, or good works the more excellent way, apart from love.

MIND, REPRESENTING KNOWLEDGE
AND THE INTELLECTUAL POWERS

Again, this chapter refers to understanding and thinking as a child; to knowing now in part, but hereafter in full; to knowing the future in prophecy; understanding all mysteries of the present; having all knowledge of the past. But the apostle does not find in the operations and possessions of the mind the more excellent way.

HEART, THE CENTRAL SOURCE
OF MORAL AND SPIRITUAL ENERGY

We have noted that the heart's proper expression is love, channeled through soul, strength, and mind. This love is not sporadic, but constant — the organizing principle of all of life in its varied relationships of feeling, thought, and action. Note — in Corinthians 13 — the characteristics of this love as it operates in these three areas: It suffereth long and is kind; it vaunteth not itself, is not puffed up; seeketh not her own; is not easily provoked; thinketh no evil; doth not behave unseemly; rejoiceth not in iniquity but in the truth; beareth, believeth, hopeth, endureth — and never fails!

Thus we see that Christian love, flowing out of man's central self, the *heart,* saturates the *soul* with pure affections and desires; directs the *strength* in full obedience and sacrificial service; and disciplines the mind in sound moral judgments.

THE FLOW OF LOVE IS RELEASED BY FAITH

Christian devotion, then, means involvement of the entire being of man in loyalty to Jesus Christ,

130

and not the exercise of some specialized religious capacity of personality. It is more than piety, which may be but a meticulous legalism with no kinship to genuine spirituality — merely a dutiful regard for the form of godliness without the power thereof.

For more than a decade of anguished quest following his graduation from Oxford, John Wesley tried this route of legalism and loaded himself heavily with good works. Following his return voyage from his disappointing missionary venture in the Georgia Colony he wrote:

> I think, verily, if the Gospel be true, I am safe: for I not only have given, and do give, all my goods to feed the poor; I not only give my body to be burned, drowned, or whatever God shall appoint for me; but I follow after charity (though not as I ought, but yet as I can) if haply I might attain it ... Whoever sees me, sees I would be a Christian ... But in a storm I think, "What if the Gospel be not true?" ... O! who will deliver me from this fear of death?

John Wesley also tried the way of ritualism in this earlier period of his life. He attempted to discover from ancient sources the rites of the Apostolic Church, thinking that to restore those rites would clear the channel of God's grace to his harried and distraught soul. In this pursuit, he practiced infant immersion in the Georgia wilderness — trine immersion at that! And on one occasion he refused the sacrament to a Moravian preacher whose baptism had not been episcopally administered.

For a time, Wesley also followed mysticism in which the emotional quality of religious experience turns inward upon the self and becomes an effort through feeling to find God, rather than the outflowing expression of emotion at having found Him. He once wrote his brother, "I think the rock on which I had nearest made shipwreck of faith was the writings of the mystics." This, from the Wesley who soon thereafter was to experience the warm heart of spiritual religion! But his warm heart was his emotional response to a personal relationship to God established by faith, and not an attempted ascent to mystical union with God. This distinction between personal experience and mystical experience is an important one.

In his later university and post-university days, Wesley traveled for a time the way of rationalism. As an Oxford undergraduate his bent toward rationalism had disturbed his father who wrote him that he liked his way of thinking and arguing, but that it frightened him. "He who wishes to cramp Revelation to his puny reason is half-Deist, half-heretic," said the father, and added, "My dear child, keep your boat between the Scylla and Charybdis." In this connection it is interesting to note that only a few years later John Wesley, when Fellow of Lincoln College, Oxford, was assigned the duty of presiding at disputations — as a debate coach, we might say today. His was a logical mind, and at this period of his life easily became prey to the snare of rationalism.

We have now noted that in Wesley's later youth and early maturity there appeared all the major distortions of devotion that men mistake for true devotion when they follow paths of their own choosing in their efforts to find and to serve God. But in none of these ways did Wesley find God; not in the sheer intellectual effort of the Oxford logician; nor in the fuzzy subjectivism of the mystic's moods; nor yet in the ritualist's adherence to the forms of the Church's hoary past; nor even in the legalist's arduous and compulsive efforts through asceticism and good works. And no more can we arrive at genuine devotion today by way of the rationalist's logic, the mystic's devotion, the ritualist's rubrics, the legalist's labors.

How, then, does one find God? The answer is simple: by faith, even as at last John Wesley found Him; by faith as a personal relationship to God through Jesus Christ as the way, the truth, and the life. Salvation comes not by the exercise of the capacities of our *soul* in feeling, of our *strength* in human effort, of our *mind* in profound thought. Salvation comes through God's work in the *heart,* wrought in response to our upward reach of faith. When the *heart* thus responds to truth, all our capacities of *soul, strength,* and *mind* are united in loyal devotion to God as the object of our trust and love. Until a man responds with his entire being to God's offer of saving grace, he has not reached the way of full devotion to Jesus Christ as Lord and Master. Could less than the united self grasp the truth, that truth would be but partial and therefore, in measure, a dangerous error. Hence arise the aberrations of religious faith that find expression in the many cults of our day that have been selective in matters of truth, denying one or more essentials of the way, the truth, and the life.

We should never forget that this faith by which

we are saved and kept is not of ourselves, but is the gift of God. Not only does man seek God, but God first seeks man. When the downward reach of the mighty Spirit of God comes to grips with the upward reach of the spirit of penitent man, then man knows by faith as the response of his inmost, utmost self to the call of God.

John Wesley made the response of faith on a May evening in 1738 when he was thrity-five years of age, and after he had followed in vain many roads of his own choosing. You are familiar with the event as he recorded it in his *Journal* for generations to come to read:

> In the evening I went very unwillingly to a society in Aldersgate Street, where one was reading Luther's preface to the Epistle to the Romans. About a quarter before nine, while he was describing the change which God works in the heart through faith in Christ, I felt my heart strangely warmed. I felt I did trust in Christ, Christ alone for salvation, and an assurance was given me, that he had taken away *my* sins, even *mine,* and saved me from the law of sin and death.

But someone asks, according to this testimony of Wesley himself, was not feeling the central fact in his experience of salvation? Certainly it was a factor, we answer, but not the essential factor. Note that this very testimony points away from himself to "faith" and "trust" in Christ. But the evidence is even stronger. An hour or so after his conversion he visited his brother Charles in the latter's sick-room. Charles in his *Journal* reports that upon entering the room John announced, "I believe." Here is no reference to feeling. The brothers then sang together a hymn Charles had just written in celebration of his own victory of faith three days earlier. One stanza of this hymn brings together the two emphases, the *feeling* of experience and the *knowledge* of faith. When true to its founding genius, Methodism still maintains this synthesis of faith and experience. The stanza may be found in *Hymns of the Living Faith,* No. 204. [This hymn is also found in *Hymns of Faith and Life,* No. 272.] I quote it:

> O how shall I the goodness tell,
>   Father, which thou to me hast showed?
> That I, a child of wrath and hell,
>   I should be called a child of God,
> Should *know,* should *feel* my sins forgiven,
>   Blest with this antepast of heav'n!

John Wesley's "warm heart" was the result of his contact with God; it was the human response to the touch of the Divine, and not the cause or the essence of that touch.

THE FLOW OF LOVE IS DIRECTED BY LAW

John Wesley taught that "faith working by love" is the essence of Christian perfection. But there are those today who distort the place of love in its application to moral and ethical situations, claiming that love alone is sufficient and the Christian need not be subject to law. These would say that Christian love needs no restraint, so let it flow where it will with no instruction in doctrine, no direction of ethics, no regulation of the affections. Such would hold that it is folly to talk about commitment to Jesus Christ as something to which matters of Christian belief and Christian living are particularly relevant; that there need be no restraining banks — only the stream of constantly shifting experience.

Someone has said that there is no logic so compelling as the logic of an eddy except a knowledge of the river. Even some who call themselves Christian are caught in "a dizzy whirl about a central emptiness," and, circling in their fragile canoe with the swirling eddy, mistakenly think they are navigating the river. Recognizing no eternally abiding principles of right and wrong, and permitting the circumstance of the moment to determine their course of action, they are poorly prepared for that crisis of temptation when the eddy grows to become a whirlpool. Their mood is akin to that existentialism which is at the heart of our decadent culture in all areas — education, literature, art, music, politics, morals, and religion. Its adherents range from philosophers, theologians and literati in respectable circles of society, to the unwed alliance of a couple of beatniks, occupying a disheveled attic bedroom and living by moment to moment impulse.

In the magazine *Christianity Today* appeared an article that uncovered the ethical anarchy of so-called Christian existentialism's emphasis on love as the adequate guide to conduct. Therein I found these pertinent words of Horatius Bonar, the hymn writer: "Love is not a rule, but a motive. Love does not tell us what to do; it tells us how to do it. Love constrains me to do the will of the loved one; but to know what that will is I must go elsewhere."

Where must I go to find the will of God? John Wesley answers:

> I am a creature of a day, passing through life, as an arrow through the air. I am a spirit come from God, and returning to God: just hovering over the great gulf; till a moment hence, I am no more seen! I drop into an unchangeable eternity! I want to know one thing, the way to heaven: how to land safe on that happy shore. God himself has condescended to teach the way; for this end he came from heaven. He hath written it down in a book! O give me that book! At any price, give me the book of God!*

You and I have that Book, in which, if we read it, we find inscribed what we should believe about the One we love and what we should do to obey Him.

THE RIVER IS ETERNAL

Supreme devotion to God directs us to His Word as a chart by which our love finds its channel that leads at last to the throne of God. There, as revealed in the Word, the Christian one day shall stand with a great multitude which no man can number — a multitude gathered of all nations, and kindreds, and people, and tongues, who have washed their robes and made them white in the blood of the Lamb. And these shall cry with a loud voice, "Salvation to our God which sitteth upon the throne, and unto the Lamb." And they shall serve God day and night in His temple, and God shall share His dwelling place with them. No more shall they hunger nor thirst, nor shall the sun or any heat light upon them. And God shall wipe away all tears from their eyes. And the

---

*This quotation from Wesley has been added by the speaker in editing the sermon for publication.

Lamb shall feed them and lead them unto living fountains of water, for "There is a river, the streams whereof shall make glad the city of God, the holy place of the tabernacles of the most High."

God's love and justice
"must be held in equipoise."

The Continental Divide in Christian Doctrine

In the nature and being of God, which has preeminence? God's justice or His love? The answer to this question sets the direction of one's theology towards Calvinism or Arminianism.

The Calvinist, in his forensic system of thinking (as in a court procedure), makes much of the justice and the righteousness of God. In the light of God's absolute righteousness and justice, man is in corruption and wickedness, even under grace.

Because man has no righteousness and is incapable of good, his righteousness is imputed to him, as a credit secured for him through Christ's righteousness, and is not an imparted or implanted righteousness.

The man of sin remains in the heart and continues to battle with the new man in Christ until death brings deliverance. It is on the basis of this belief that, in extreme developments of Calvinism, some men have held the belief that continuing in sin makes grace to abound.

By this, they mean that the Christian's violation of the law, that is, his sinning, glorifies God by revealing the inexhaustible store of God's grace through Christ's suffering for him on the Cross. Thus, the sinning believer says to God the Father, in effect, "Charge my sin to the account of your Son's inexhaustible deposit of grace made available to me through His death on the Cross."

The Apostle Paul writes of this in Romans 3:31, "Do we then make void the law through faith?" This is known in the history of doctrine as *antinomianism,* the word meaning "against law." Those holding this view maintain that the believer is made free from the law's requirement.

John Wesley encountered this doctrine more than two centuries ago. In his *Journal* under a 1746 date, he reported his conversation with a man who when Wesley asked him if he believed he had nothing to do with the law, replied, "I am not under the law: I live by faith." Then Wesley asked, "Have you, as living by faith, a right to everything in the world?" He answered, "I have; all is mine since Christ is mine." And he further asserted that this was true of the possessions of others — they were his, and even the bodies of consenting women. Wesley asked him if this was not sin, and his answer was, "Yes, to him that thinks it is a sin; but not to those whose hearts are free." In righteous indignation, Wesley exclaimed, in his *Journal,* against such perverters of the gospel, "Surely these are the firstborn children of Satan."

According to Calvinism, what is the nature of the atonement? It is in the nature of a court action, that is, forensic or legal. It is objectively accomplished the moment I confess Christ and believe on Him. I become a Christian by endorsing a contract, assenting to Christ's paying the price of my sins on Calvary. Thereby God's justice is satisfied for my sins — past, present, and future — and I can write checks at will on His infinite provisions of grace, and the Father will honor them! Christ is a cover for sin, not a cure.

According to this view, my righteousness is not actual, only positional. If I am in Christ, I am clothed with His righteousness. When God looks upon my sins through Christ's blood, He does not see my sins! The meaning of this view for ethics is readily apparent. In their emphasis on forensic or legal union with Christ, these extremists neglect ethical union with Christ, and they are likely to become careless in matters of Christian conduct.

If the justice of God overshadows His love, then man is ethically hopeless, and with a free conscience may sin daily in word, thought, and deed.

We are not to think that all Calvinists have carried to such excess the implications some have drawn from its underlying concepts anymore than have all Arminians accepted the way-out liberalism of some Arminians.

The tradition of Methodism, following John Wesley, is Arminianism warmed by Wesley's emphasis on an inner experience of grace which goes far deeper than the intellectual assent of Calvinism. Its pull is subjective in contrast with the Calvinist's objective emphasis. A fair comparison is brought out in the two views on the two doctrinal patterns regarding *total depravity*.

TOTAL DEPRAVITY

Calvinism's view holds that in man — apart from grace — there is naught but corruption and, as we have previously mentioned, maintains that the old man of sin continues an unceasing warfare until death releases the soul of the believer.

But the Arminian doctrine concerning *total depravity* holds that whereas in man, apart from grace, there is nothing by which, of himself by nature, he can merit God's favor and his soul's salvation, there are qualities in the natural man upon which grace can work. This milder view has led some to the humanistic position that there is a resident goodness in man's nature which can by nurture develop into Christian character.

Thus, moral ethics, which stress man's own righteousness, takes the place of atonement for sin among some Arminians, who idealize human nature and hold that eventually man's progress will bring the millennium of a perfect social order. But this dream of Arminian liberalism has been shattered by the moral corruption so evident today in the human condition the world around.

And some, nevertheless, have taken the further step to universalism, believing that someday, somehow, all mankind will be saved. Arminianism can, therefore, tend to let the love of God overshadow God's justice and righteousness.

We began our remarks with the question, "Which has preeminence in the nature and essential being of God — His justice or His love? Have we arrived at an answer? If God is essentially neither justice nor love, what is He? If neither the logic of rigid Calvinism nor the subjectiveness of Arminianism is the answer, then where do we turn for an answer?

The answer is both God's justice and His love! We must balance on the continent's ridge — may we call it the Continental Divide in Christian doctrine? The justice of God and the love of God must be held in

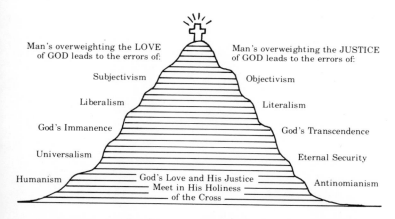

Man's overweighting the LOVE of GOD leads to the errors of:

Man's overweighting the JUSTICE of GOD leads to the errors of:

Subjectivism — Objectivism
Liberalism — Literalism
God's Immanence — God's Transcendence
Universalism — Eternal Security
Humanism — Antinomianism

God's Love and His Justice Meet in His Holiness of the Cross

THE CONTINENTAL DIVIDE IN CHRISTIAN DOCTRINE

As Christians move nearer the Cross of Jesus Christ in which are displayed in perfect harmony both God's Justice and His Love, they move nearer one another, and their differences diminish. The equipoise of *love* and *justice* in God's dealings with mankind leans neither toward the cold, legal atonement of historic Calvinism and its extreme of Antinomianism on the right, nor toward Arminianism's drift to liberal humanism and its extreme of Universalism on the left. God' transcendence and His immanence are a balanced synthesis.

equipoise: love, the moving of God toward man and the motive of all His dealings with man; justice and righteousness, the regulating principle controlling even God's love in its expression.

"Let love be your guide" is a pernicious motto. Love is not a guide, not a controlling principle. *Love is a motive!* But motive needs direction, which means knowledge and discernment.

In the Cross are both God's love, moving Him toward man, and also His justice demanding satisfaction for sin. Loving man, God would save Him; but He cannot violate His own justice. The Cross satisfies that justice.

The holiness message
at its best, simplest, clearest.
Reprinted by permission, The Holiness Pulpit
Beacon Hill Press, 1957
Compiled by James McGraw

What It Means to Love God Perfectly

Thou shalt love the Lord thy God with all thy heart, and with all thy soul, and with all thy strength, and with all thy mind; and thy neighbor as thyself.

Luke 10:27

In the chapter preceding our scripture lesson, I Corinthians 13, the Apostle Paul gives an account of Christian gifts and graces, and then declares that he will point out a way more excellent than all these. Accordingly, in our lesson he sets forth the more excellent way as the way of love. Such also is the emphasis of our text. In fact, I Corinthians 13 is an expansion of our text's terse but comprehensive outline of man's relationships to God and to his neighbor. Note how naturally the chapter's units of thought group themselves under the four aspects of man's essential nature as given in Luke 10:27. We consider them in a somewhat reversed order of their listing in our text:

Strength, expressed in action, conduct, and service. In this connection, the chapter refers to speaking with tongues of men and angels, giving all one's goods to feed the poor, giving one's body to be burned, moving mountains by the power of faith. But Paul does not find in action and service the more excellent way.

Mind, representing man's knowledge and intellectual powers. The chapter refers to understanding and thinking as a child, knowing now in part but hereafter in full, knowing the future in prophecy, understanding the mysteries of the present, having all knowledge of the past. But Paul does not find in knowledge the more excellent way.

Soul, standing for the feeling or affectional nature. From this chapter's enumeration of the soul's affections and desires, we observe that the more excellent way consists not in a superficial stirring of the emotions, not in an ecstasy of the moment, nor yet in a sustained mood of pleasure.

Heart, as the central source of moral and spiritual energy. The heart is the essential self, which, loving God perfectly, channels its energy of love through *soul, mind,* and *strength.* Love becomes the organizing principle of the entire being, issuing from the heart as the central spring of life and flowing through all man's relationships of feeling, thought, and action. According to our lesson, this love suffereth long, is kind, vaunteth not self, is not puffed up, seeketh not her own, is not provoked, thinketh no evil, does not behave unseemly, rejoiceth not in iniquity but in the truth, beareth, believeth, hopeth, endureth — and never fails!

Man's first duty is to love God from his inmost, utmost being, out of that deepest spring of all his energies, the *heart;* and then to yield every area of his redeemed personality to the outrush of love: the whole *mind* in pure thoughts and disciplined judgment; the entire *strength* in righteous conduct and obedient service; all the *soul* in pure affections and holy desires. This is the more excellent way.*

And this more excellent way is what John Wesley called Christian perfection: no more and no less! This perfection is not a perfection of knowledge, nor of emotional mood, nor yet of conduct. It is a heart of pure love for God and man. In the man who loves God perfectly and his neighbor as himself, the trend or current of life's energies is Godward, with no angry crosscurrents toward sin, no swirling eddies rotating about hollow, selfish centers, but the sweep of a mighty tide to the ocean of God's holiness.

Why do good people resist such a teaching that Christians may be holy in heart and purpose in this life? Partly because those claiming the experience are sometimes led by enthusiasm into overstatement in testimony or are carried away by rhapsody in preaching; in part also because critics of the doctrine set up a "straw man,"overstating our claims the more easily to refute them. John Wesley said that Christian perfection "must be disguised . . . covered with a bearskin" before it can be opposed. Let the friends of Christian perfection see that they spread no "bearskin" over it!

THE PERFECTION OF LOVE, NOT PERFECTION UNDER THE LAW

The perfection Christians may reach in this life is

---

*For illuminating comments on Luke 10:27, see John Wesley's *Explanatory Notes upon the New Testament* and Weymouth's *New Testament in Modern Speech* (enlarged Fifth Edition).

not a legal perfection. Adam's perfection before he sinned was the perfection of complete obedience to God's perfect law, an obedience made possible because Adam had come from the creative hand of God, in God's unmarred image, with perfect powers of body and mind. But there are mars and scars even in a saint because of sin in the race and sin in his earlier unregenerate life; and these scars will persist until he knows "the power of his resurrection." These infirmities prevent his perfect conformity in this life to the demands of God's absolute will.

It cannot be God's perfect will that I offend my brother, but with purest motive and a heart of love, I do sometimes offend him! A man one time employed under my supervision in the work of the church had plunged his department into a serious financial deficit through error in judgment. There was no question concerning his personal honesty. In a committee called to consider the problem, I attempted to relieve the embarrassment my brother suffered by a carefully phrased statement. This statement miscarried, and what I had intended as balm to his hurt only wounded him the more deeply.

Our perfection, then, is not a legal perfection but a perfection of heart, of motive, of intent, of love. Fully willing the perfect law of God, our failure to meet that law comes, not from any rivalry within of sin or self set against God's will, but from infirmities entailed by the blight of sin in the race and our own unregenerate years. As Daniel Steele once put it, "All there is left of us, after sin has spread its blight, may be filled with the fullness of God."

THE PERFECTION OF GROWTH,
NOT THE PERFECTION OF ETERNITY

They err who attempt to refute the doctrine and to discredit the experience of Christian perfection with Paul's statement that he had not attained, neither was already perfect (see Philippians 3:12). From the context it is clear that Paul is here writing of the perfection of the resurrection. He further declares that right now, in this life, he is stretching toward the goal of eternity. This goal for Paul was not an entrance into heaven "through gates ajar," but attainment "unto the measure of the stature of the fulness of Christ" (Ephesians 4:13), toward which goal he would increase through the cycles of eternity.

We can never reach in this life the perfection that will be ours in eternity. But if we follow the teaching and example of Paul, we will strive toward that perfection in this life. This means no resting on our oars, no leaning back on some past experience, but growing constantly in grace and in knowledge of the truth as we strive in time toward the goal of eternity.

Note the words of John as he looked forward to a perfection we cannot know in this life:

> Beloved, now are we the sons of God, and it doth not yet appear what we shall be: but we know that, when he shall appear, we shall be like him; for we shall see him as he is. And every man that hath this hope in him purifieth himself, even as he is pure.   I John 3:2-3

In similar vein, Paul wrote in our scripture lesson:

> Now we see through a glass, darkly; but then face to face: now I know in part; but then shall I know even as also I am known.　　　　　　　　　I Corinthians 13:12

But if our perfection in this life is not the perfection we will reach in eternity, is it then something less than perfection? No, for the perfection of the Christian here is never something less than perfection in quality — that would not be perfection at all! There is a perfection of the blade, then of the ear, and after that of the full corn in the ear. The apple blossom may be perfect in quality but not complete or perfect in development or maturity, for the fulfillment of its purpose is consummated only in the ripened apple. There is a perfection of bud, bloom, and fruit, each in quality no less perfect than another. The doctor declares a newborn babe "a perfect child" although it lacks the size, proportions, and powers of the fully matured man.

Always, then, that holiness of heart — which means perfection of love — is complete in quality while there remain vast areas of growth and wider application of what it means to love God perfectly. Perfection of love begins as an act and continues as a process. When Paul said, "Let us cleanse ourselves from all filthiness of the flesh and spirit, perfecting holiness in the fear of God" (II Corinthians 7:1), he did not mean a continuous washing, never consummated in cleanness. The Greek tense here used for *cleanse* means an act of completed cleansing. Paul admirably combines in this one statement an exhortation to instantaneous and completed cleansing with an exhortation to continuing growth in holiness. Here we have both crisis and process. The

150

instantaneous, inward cleansing is to be worked out in daily living as we apply perfect love more and more completely to all areas of our lives. The one who loves God perfectly ever grows in grace and in a knowledge of the truth.

PERFECT LOVE BUT IMPERFECT LIVES

Why are there imperfections in the lives of those who love God perfectly? We have answered this question in principle, but now we would be more specific.

In all behavior that has moral meaning, we must reckon with three factors. There is first *the impulse to action.* In the unregenerate, the impulse of nature is toward evil; in the carnal, there are angry crosscurrents toward sin. But in him who loves God perfectly, the tide of the soul is Godward, for he fully wills the perfect will of God.

Next is the factor of *judgment.* In no one is the understanding perfect, and an imperfect mind may betray a pure heart into mistakes that thwart God's perfect law. The grace of God does improve the Christian's thinking powers by bringing rest of soul, eagerness to study that he may better know God's will, and release from the drag of evil habits of mind and body. But God's grace does not perfect the eye of the mind nor cleanse the atmosphere through which light must reach it. Indeed, "Now we see through a glass, darkly." Native mentality and past experience will ever be present to influence in measure even a saint's moral judgment. A sinner may surpass a saint in mental capacity and in opportunities from past training to discriminate right and wrong in certain difficult and complex situations. "Unto whomsoever much is given, of him shall much be required" (Luke 12:48).

Furthermore, once the moral end has been fixed, whether by impulse or by reason, there remains for consideration the person's *ability to reach the end.* Again in this, the sinner may surpass the saint because of past experience in the area involved or because of greater intellectual or physical ability.

A wicked man is angry with his neighbor. The impulse of his nature is to destroy him. He is a clever man and cunningly plots his neighbor's destruction. He carefully studies his neighbor's habits and discovers that on a certain night each week the neighbor has an appointment in the nearby village, making the journey by a lonely footpath through his pasture. He consults the almanac to find the dark of the moon. He carefully prepares his gun. On the chosen night, he hides in a thicket only a few feet from the neighbor's path. At the expected time, the unsuspecting neighbor approaches; and at the moment of his passing, the evil man presses the trigger — but his gun jams and the neighbor's life is spared! Nevertheless, the evil man is a murderer! Not before the law, but before God he is as truly a murderer as though his neighbor's life had flowed away in the dust at his feet. Applying the three factors found in all moral conduct to this case, we note that a clever intellect cunningly plotted the design by which an evil impulse should be consummated; the evil man failed to reach this wicked end only by a circumstance beyond his control.

On the other hand, note a good man's failure to accomplish a good end. Crossing a bridge over a turbulent stream, he hears the desperate cry of a man caught in the angry current. The impulse of his nature is to rescue the drowning man even at the risk of his own life. He rushes to the river's edge, throws off his outer garments, and plunges into the current. As he swims toward the drowning man, he calls to mind all he has learned about proper approach and method of pinioning a drowning man's arms to escape their grip of desperation. But notwithstanding his benevolent impulse, his careful planning of the attempted rescue, and his marshaling all his physical powers for this crisis, he is caught in the floundering man's vice-like grip; and both men sink in the stream. In time their bodies are brought to shore, and methods of resuscitation are applied. One man revives — he is the would-be rescuer. The other man is dead. But the would-be rescuer nevertheless is a hero, deserving praise even as though he had succeeded in his effort. The "set of his soul" was beneficient; he drew upon every power of body and mind to save the other. But his strength and skill were inadequate.

FULFILLING THE LAW OF LOVE

If through lack of knowledge, impaired judgment, or limited powers of body or mind, I fail to meet God's perfect will, must I then accept my failure without protest and without effort to overcome the infirmity? Here is the failure of so many, that they offend the law of love by heeding not the effect of their infirmities upon others. The infirmity is the occasion of sin when I care not that it offends my brother. If I love God with a perfect heart and my neighbor as myself, I will take toward the offense I unwittingly give, the same steps to restore fellowship with my offended brother, which I ought to take if I had willfully wronged him and later sought restoration to God's favor. Man cannot be right with God and knowingly be wrong with man!

A friend of mine was superintendent of a racial group in his church's home missions department. This group had arranged a great convention and lavishly decorated a large hall for the event. Then the superintendent was invited to survey their arrangements. My friend was of an artistic temperament whose aesthetic and cultural standards differed from those of the racial group he served. With the chairman of the decorating committee, he entered the hall that had been so profusely decorated with clashing colors. The moment he entered, his delicately adjusted nervous system violently recoiled from the pain to his aesthetic sensibilities, and he exclaimed his displeasure. The other man, who had made this task a labor of love, was deeply wounded and soon withdrew from the fellowship of his group, secluding himself in his little cottage.

My friend, who had unintentionally inflicted the wound, might have wrapped himself smugly in a cloak of righteous motive, blaming the other as carnal to take offense when he himself had meant no wrong. But instead, he called the leaders of the group and confessed to them how he had wronged his brother and asked their help in winning back the offended one. After repeated efforts at reconciliation, the superintendent succeeded in restoring the man's confidence, and thus the man was renewed in fellowship with the Christian group and strengthened in his relationship to God.

But is the distinction between sin and infirmity a valid one? It is, indeed! Failing to make this distinction leads even Christians to say that they sin daily in word, thought, and deed. Moral confusion results when infirmities are called sins, along with willful violations of God's known law. On the other hand, when we make this necessary distinction, there is the subtle danger that some who profess to love God perfectly will plead infirmities to excuse their offenses, resting in the innocence of their motives while neglecting the evil consequences of the miscarriage of their good intentions. Thus they may land in an "inverted eternal security" whose argument is not, "I have accepted Christ, and therefore I can never be lost," but is the equally erroneous logic of "I am saved and sanctified, and therefore nothing I do can be wrong."

Our protection against such error is faithfully to follow our Lord's instruction:

> Therefore if thou bring thy gift to the altar, and there rememberest that thy brother hath ought against thee; leave there thy gift before the altar, and go thy way; first be reconciled to thy brother, and then come and offer thy gift.
> Matthew 5:23-24

What an outrush of love would follow upon the general observance of this command among Christians! That tide of love would melt down coldness and break through barriers that have divided brethren. And then, throughout the church, would come revival.

* * *

Brethren in this message we have tried to remove the ''bearskin'' that too often has disguised the doctrine and experience of Christian perfection, showing its true shape as nothing higher or lower than Wesley's claim that it means loving God with all the heart, mind, soul, and strength, and loving one's neighbor as oneself. In Wesley's own words, ''It is love governing the heart and life, running through all our tempers, words and actions.''

We close with the benediction of Jude, paraphrased as suggested by Dr. Steele to distinguish deliverance from sin now and deliverance from infirmities hereafter:

> Now unto Him that is able to keep you from sinning in this life, and to present you without infirmity in the presence of His glory with exceeding joy, to the only wise God our Saviour, be glory and majesty, dominion and power, both now and ever. Amen.

Faith Working by Love

A scribe asked Jesus, What is the chief commandment? His reply declared it to be man's primary adjustment to God through a love that harmonizes all man's powers with God's will. This is the vertical reach of religion. But Jesus added the second commandment, by which He declared man's proper relationship to His brother as the horizontal or social reach of love. There is no commandment greater than these two: the heart-center of our holy religion, therefore, is a love that reaches upward to God and outward to man.

These two commandments confront us with that problem which for long centuries has perplexed and divided the Christian church: the place of faith versus works as man's part in his salvation.

Our present inquiry seeks to clarify the scriptural synthesis of faith and works as set forth by John Wesley, to trace the social direction of historic Methodism, and to define the problem of social Christianity for our day.

WESLEY ON FAITH AND WORKS

In his *Explanatory Notes on the New Testament,* John Wesley in a single statement, most difficult to

157

surpass, summarizes the relationship of faith and works as taught by Scripture:

> Works do not give life to faith, but faith begets works and then is perfected in them.

In another connection Wesley well expressed his position. To correct a critic's misunderstanding of one of his preachers as teaching salvation by works, he wrote:

> None of us talk of being accepted for our works; that is the Calvinist slander. But we all maintain we are not saved without works, that works are a condition (though not the meritorious cause) of final salvation.
> *Letters of John Wesley,* vol. 6, p. 76

On another occasion he defended a preacher against the charge of teaching sanctification through works, saying:

> Probably the difference between you and others lies in words chiefly. All who expect to be sanctified at all expect to be sanctified by faith. But meantime they know that faith will not be given but to them that obey. Remotely, therefore, the blessing depends on our works, although immediately upon simple faith.
> *Letters,* vol. 4, p. 71

John Wesley made much of the social direction of the Christian religion, good works being the fruit of a living faith and a condition of one's continuing in a personal relationship to God. But he protested vigorously against works as the basis of merit for salvation. Note this statement in his sermon, "Salvation by Faith."

> For there is nothing we are, or have, or do, which can deserve the least thing at God's hand. . . . And whatever righteousness may be found in man, this is also the gift of God.   Wesley's *Works,* vol. 9, 5th ed., 1860

By this deliberate statement, one must then judge Wesley's teachings on social Christianity as making good works the fruit of a vital faith, a "faith working by love."

Perhaps nowhere did he more strongly declare the social character of Christianity than in these words:

> The gospel of Christ knows of no religion, but social; no holiness but social holiness. Faith working by love is the length and breadth and depth and height of Christian perfection.   *Works,* vol. 7, p. 393

SOCIAL CONCERN IN ACTION

In his own life, Wesley exemplified well his precepts urging to good works, and they found expression likewise in the "societies" he founded and directed for more than a half century. He established the first dispensary in London, opened workshops for the unemployed poor, built a benevolent loan fund, and collected a charity fund out of which to aid the needy who were not members of a Methodist society. When past eighty, one cold winter he trudged the streets of London in ankle-deep snow and slush to collect two hundred pounds with which to buy clothes for the poor. In consequence, he became ill from the exposure.

He was active in social reform, promoting temperance, opposing slavery, condemning political corruption, analyzing the relationship of luxury to poverty, exposing the folly of war, and holding up a standard against such common evils of the days as gambling and smuggling.

But Wesley's hope was not to reform society by the application of peripheral patches to its open sores; but it was to change the hearts and lives of individuals by which social healing would come from personal soundness. Therefore, his primary method of social reform was religious revival, and this method brought astounding social consequences.

Within a few months after the outbreak of revival under Whitefield in the degraded Kingswood area, Wesley reported the social and moral change as follows:

> Kingswood does not now, as a year ago, resound with cursing and blasphemy. It is no more filled with drunkenness, and the idle diversions that naturally lead thereto. It is no longer full of wars and fightings, of clamour and bitterness, of wrath and envyings. Peace and love are there.

A similar change came to West Cornwall which long had been a region of smugglers, fighters, and those who lured ships on the rocks to plunder them. A year after revival struck that neighborhood, there was not a single felon in its prison. Charles Wesley said this had not been known before in the memory of man.

But the social benefits of revival were more than local in scope; they were national. The times were morally desperate. *The Cambridge Modern History* characterizes the period thus:

160

> The earlier half of the eighteenth century was an age of materialism, a period of dim ideals and expiring hopes.
>
> Vol. 6, p. 76

In 1738, the very year of John Wesley's "heartwarming," Bishop Berkeley in his *Discourse to Magistrates and Men in Authority* declared,

> Morality and religion have collapsed to a degree that has never been known in any Christian country!

England had been caught in the current that swept France to violent revolution later in the century. How do you explain England's escape from such a bloodbath as came to France? According to historians, the explanation lies in the reforming effect of the evangelical revival upon England's masses. Even such a historian as Lecky, who had no great sympathy for vital religion, has set the pattern for other historians in his affirmation that "Wesley saved England from the French Revolution." Although seeming to give the history of the Methodist movement every possible unfavorable twist, at the same time Lecky gives high praise to the social and moral reformation it achieved. Of the Aldersgate experience of John Wesley he wrote, "It is scarcely an exaggeration to say that the scene which took place in that humble meeting in Aldersgate Street forms an epoch in English history."

JOHN WESLEY ON SOCIAL ISSUES

In *Thoughts on the Present Scarcity of Provisions,* Wesley blamed lack of bread on the use of corn for distilling liquors; lack of oats on feeding the horses of the rich; lack of mutton and beef on the breeding of horses for the rich and for export to France. His proposed remedies: Prohibit distilling; tax luxury goods heavily; discontinue useless pensions and pay the national debt.

Concerning fair-trade practices he wrote:

> We cannot, consistent with brotherly love, sell our goods below market price; we cannot study to ruin our neighbor's trade to advance our own.

Thirteen years before the Abolition Committee was organized in England to combat slavery, and while this evil was flourishing under the law, Wesley wrote *Thoughts Upon Slavery,* wherein he said:

> Can human law turn darkness into light or evil into good? Notwithstanding ten thousand laws, right is right and wrong is wrong. . . . I deny that villainy is ever necessary; a man can be under no necessity of degrading himself into a wolf. . . . Give liberty to whom liberty is due, that is to every child of man, to every partaker of human nature. Let none serve you but by his own voluntary choice.

And to Wilberforce, in the last letter Wesley ever wrote, he called slavery "that sum of all villainies." Concerning the liquor traffic he wrote:

> Neither may we gain by hurting our neighbor in his body. Therefore we may not sell anything which tends to impair health; such is evidently that liquid fire, commonly called drams or spirituous liquors.

In speaking of the war of the American Revolution he wrote an indictment of all wars:

But a matter is in dispute relative to the mode of taxation. So these countrymen, children of the same parents, are to *murder* each other in all possible haste — to *prove* who is in the right. What an argument is this! What a method of proof! What an amazing way of deciding controversies!

WESLEY'S SOCIAL PRINCIPLES CRITICIZED

Notwithstanding the generally acknowledged benefits accruing to society from the Wesleyan Revival, there are today severe critics of Wesley's social views and methods. Maldwyn Edwards, in *After Wesley,* decries the conservative effect of his teaching on Christian perfection in terms so exclusively personal as not to provoke in his followers a proper concern for society.

This criticism is difficult to accept as applied to Wesley's own definition and elaboration of the doctrine and experience of Christian perfection, however well the criticism might apply to some of Wesley's followers, especially after Wesley's death. Wesley himself emphasized the social direction of Christianity with a force and clarity few modern prophets have achieved. Both in principle and in application, he held love in sharp focus. His making I Corinthians 13 the pattern of Christian perfection, his extensive exposition of works in their relationship to faith in his *Notes* on James, his "General Rules for the United Societies," his sermons, his personal example — all these give vigorous thrust to the horizontal reach of "faith working by love."

And yet, H. Richard Niebuhr, in *The Social Sources of Denominationalism,* gives John Wesley small credit for a sensitive social conscience. Here is

Niebuhr's viewpoint:

> The social ethics of Methodism was an ethics of philanthropy and humanitarianism, which regarded movements toward equality as concessions made out of love rather than as demands of justice, and this philanthropy suffered the constant danger of degenerating into sentimental charity. But the typical social ethics of the poor is an ethics of reconstruction whose excrescencies appear in violence rather than in sentimentality.

It is astounding that those who criticize Wesley's source of social concern, Christian love, discount love in favor of violence and revolution as the method of social reform. Turning to the Scriptures, particularly to the Sermon on the Mount, one finds solid support for Wesley's principle of outgoing love rather than violent and vindictive revolution.

Dr. Mary Alice Tenney, in *Blueprint for a Christian World,* points out Wesley's conflict with his times at the points of humanistic philosophy, moral compromise, and social injustice. She cites a letter Wesley wrote to Bishop Seeker stating that even before he had "preached or (known) salvation by faith," he had been excluded from several pulpits for preaching love to God and man as the substance of religion. We venture to assert that had Wesley's emphasis, at that early date or later, been mere philanthropy and humanitarianism, his preaching could hardly have aroused such antagonism. But as a prophet, his realism pricked the sensibilities of favored groups and provoked their active hostility.

In that exciting book, *A Tale of Two Brothers,* Mabel Richmond Brailsford claims that, under

Wesley's teachings, "Resignation became a prime virtue and restiveness under suffering a major crime"; and she casts aspersion on the alleged otherworldliness of early Methodism in these words:

> It has been said that when the Wesleys began their work, England was ripe for revolution, but by preaching the duty of obedience to rulers and of patience under affliction, and by representing this earthly life, with its negations and miseries, as the indispensable training ground for the heavenly, they lulled asleep the restlessness and resentment of the deeply wronged poor.

The author then attempts to support her charge with the account of the response to Charles Wesley's plea to the colliers of Kingswood when, because of the high price of bread during a period of scarcity, they were moving on Bristol as a mob. Some of them, especially converts of the Kingswood revival, turned aside to join Charles in prayer. In due time, the rest of the rioters returned from Bristol where no violence had broken out, the crowd satisfying itself that some of their leaders had presented their grievances to the mayor.

Which does Mrs. Brailsford prefer, riots or orderly negotiations? One of her severest criticisms of Methodism charges that its teachings made the lower classes docile. In fact, on this ground she charges that the Methodist revival must in part be held responsible for the social and economic evils attending England's Industrial Revolution of the following century.

But in truth, John Wesley's love was far from that docile, placid variety which lacks the strength and fiber of a sanctified will to pass judgment on evils in society or to rebuke it in the individual. And on occasion, his *Journal* records, with no hint of disapproval, instances of popular uprisings against economic justice. That his influence was effective in positive reforms, even his critics concede.

Richard Niebuhr adds to his criticism this acknowledgment:

> Methodism largely represented the religious aspect of that great revolutionary movement of the eighteenth century which placed the individual at the center of things and so profoundly modified all existing institutions.

He further states that "The Methodist revival was the last great religious revolution of the disinherited in Christendom." By this, Niebuhr means that social reforms thereafter were to be secular, even as the revolution we know today as Communism.

Maldwyn Edwards grants that "John Wesley helped to make England conscious of its social obligations" and further says:

> Yet the revival of religion did leaven Society in a clear and unmistakable manner. Gross brutality in sport disappeared: there came an improvement in the tone of the drama, and J. R. Green was able to speak of the fresh spirit of moral zeal which at the end of the eighteenth century purified our literature and our manners.

Even Mrs. Brailsford has brought herself to say, "It must be acknowledged that by inculcating the virtues of thrift and honesty he [Wesley] raised the standard of morals of the working classes, and so, almost automatically, improved their living conditions." In the second to the last paragraph of her book, she again comments favorably, saying, "Wilberforce, Shaftesbury, Howard, and a host of others less known to fame carried to their logical conclusion the tasks for which the Wesleys had prepared the way."

Viewed against the background of his century, John Wesley was far advanced in his social sensitiveness, his economic and social insights, and in his practical application of principles to the needs of society. Although his critics today would have had him seek reform by fomenting revolution, Wesley was both philanthropist and reformer. Too many reformers, concerned with abstract justice, can let multitudes suffer while they "fight for a cause." But the reformer who is moved by a sincere and Christian love, not for a particular class or order of men, but for all men as neighbors, combines philanthropy with reform and moves to help the needy victim while working for a more radical corrective through social justice.

METHODISM'S SOCIAL EMPHASIS FOLLOWING WESLEY

From its origin, Methodism has been a powerful influence in moral and social reform; but even from the closing years of Wesley's life, the struggle to maintain the ethics of love in social relationships has been acute. Its founder foresaw increase in wealth among Methodists in consequence of the sobriety, industry, and frugality engendered by the Wesleyan movement; and to guard against the softening effects of prosperity, he urged the formula: Earn all you can; save all you can; give all you can.

Notwithstanding Wesley's concern, Methodism in England early became middle class and, in measure, lost its grip on the working classes. The Conference of 1805 declared: "In some places an undue attachment to worldly business, cares and gains, with perhaps an increase in riches, prevents any growth in a heavenly and devotional spirit."

American Methodism was caught in the financial and social developments of the "gilded age" in the latter part of the nineteenth century and likewise moved rapidly to middle-class status.

In both England and America, Methodism has fluctuated in its course in such areas of social concern as pew rentals, slavery, and temperance. Even before Wesley's death, a few city chapels in England rented pews. By 1805, persons who were not pewholders found it difficult to get into the more popular London chapels. Even in pioneer America, pews were rented in the New England area early in the nineteenth century. General Conference action delayed the extension of pewed churches, resulting in policy governing the matter being left to local churches near midcentury. Thereafter, pewed churches were common in the cities. The issue was vital in the reform movement, which gave rise to the Free Methodist Church in 1860, and principally determined the naming of this new denomination of Methodists. But for generations now, free churches have been the regular order in all divisions of Methodism.

We have previously stated Wesley's position on alcoholic indulgence. In the period following his death, the English church departed far from Wesley's standard and even came to oppose the cause of total abstinence. And as Methodism in America followed the frontier, it compromised with frontier culture and accepted the use of liquor without serious protest. But both in England and in America as the nineteenth century advanced, Methodism came to the forefront in temperance reform. However, a strong minority in English Methodism carried its opposition to the cause of total abstinence into the twentieth century. And in America today it is an acknowledged fact that again many in major Methodism feel free to indulge their craving for alcohol.

American Methodism's course on the slavery issue also deviated far from the standard declared by Methodism's founder. The record is an embarrassing account of successive compromises. Economic interests in the South and ecclesiastical prudence in the North exerted damaging pressures against the original position established by the first General Conference in 1784. With the rise of the abolition movement in the North, vigorous ecclesiastical measures attempted to stifle its every appearance in Methodism. The outcome was the separation of the abolition reform group and the organization of the Wesleyan Methodist Connexion in 1843. Soon thereafter occurred the great division into a Northern and a Southern Methodism. Compromise had failed to maintain a united church.

Concerning a further issue with important social

bearings, American Methodism in general has been indifferent. Except for occasional conference resolutions against membership in lodges, the church has taken no stand against organized oath-bound secrecy. Mr. Cross, in *The Burned-Over Area*, reports as follows concerning Methodism's tolerance on the secrecy issue during the turmoil following the murder of William Morgan in 1826 (allegedly by Masons):

> Methodists appear to have been the least disturbed denomination throughout the episode. Petitions from local conferences for a church disciplinary rule on Masonic affiliation entertained no hope of passage, while in several localities individuals excluded from Presbyterian congregations on this count joined the Methodists with impunity.

Perhaps Methodism, hitherto popularly identified with frontier culture and the lower classes, now began to seek influence by "belonging." Anyway, it was clear by midcentury that Methodism was attempting to break from its frontier limitations and to achieve status among the older and more reputable denominations.

It is a matter of record that in western New York secrecy was a prominent issue leading to the separation from parent Methodism of the reform movement which in 1860 became the Free Methodist Church. The Wesleyan Methodist Connexion, which several years earlier had grown out of a slavery-reform movement, likewise came in time to establish a standard against lodge membership.

METHODISM'S TREND
TO SOCIAL CHRISTIANITY

Notwithstanding official Methodism's adjustment to standards below those declared by Wesley in certain areas of social concern, the Methodist pattern of devotion to God and of righteousness toward men continued, deeply engrained as it was in the hearts and minds of large numbers. Wesley's *General Rules,* officially accepted on both sides of the Atlantic, continued to exert strong influence on personal piety and social righteousness.

But in the closing decades of the nineteenth century in America, the hold of the *General Rules* on rank-and-file Methodism was weakened by rapid growth in membership, by the accumulation of wealth, and by increase in social status. "Culture Christianity" began to submerge the vigorous personal religion of former years. With the subsidence of the vertical or personal emphasis in the religion of Methodists, there developed a stronger horizontal or social emphasis, especially among Methodist leaders.

Timothy L. Smith, in his book *Revivalism and Social Reform,* traces the revival movement of the middle of the nineteenth century, which swept through most denominations in America in association with a strong perfectionist urge, and claims to find therein certain sources of the social gospel that came to flower at century's end. That Methodism, outstanding at midcentury both in its revivalism and in its preaching of Christian perfection, and so quickly assimilated social Christianity at century's end, lends support to Smith's claim. At any rate, in

Methodism the social gospel quickly came into favor, and in 1908 the General Conference of the Methodist Episcopal Church proclaimed its "Social Creed."

Long before the dawn of the social gospel era, however, that Methodist classic, *The Tongue of Fire,* by William Arthur (the original English edition, 1856) declared that those who expect institutions to make men good are disappointed for the reason here quoted:

> Good institutions to a certain extent presuppose a good people. Where the degree of goodness existing in the people does not, in some measure, correspond with that presupposed in the institutions, the latter can never be sustained. . . . Good institutions given to a depraved and unprincipled people, end in bringing that which is good into disrepute. . . . The only way to the effectual regeneration of society is the regeneration of individuals; make the tree good, and the fruit will be good; make good men, and you will easily found and sustain good institutions.

The shift from the personal and vertical to the institutional and horizontal in religion now has had several decades in which to produce fruit. Not all its fruit is good. Quite recently Dr. W. W. Sweet, well-known Methodist authority on American church history, has declared that the largest churches numerically have become impersonal, more interested in "causes" than in persons. We quote him on the social gospel:

> When I was a student in seminary, we were going to save the world by becoming proficient in sociology and many of us rushed over to Columbia University to take courses in sociology under Giddings. The Social Gospel

172

advocates insisted that you cannot make a better world by "snatching brands from the burning," by proceeding with the conversion of people one by one. They insisted that the Church must deal with society as a whole, with basic causes for sinful living. In their enthusiasm to save society, they overlooked sinners. Revivalism, they held, was ineffective, out of date, and must therefore be discarded.

Then World War I provided the cause of "making the world safe for democracy," but it did not succeed; peace crusades followed — and came to failure. Other causes the church has since espoused, Sweet notes, have included race relations, international relations, international justice. Then he says:

> Many who sat under such preaching no doubt were in full agreement with the preacher and agreed something should be done about it; but as far as they themselves were concerned, there was little urge for them to be better men and women.

And throughout these years, religious education has increasingly outstripped revivalism in the church's program with the result, says Sweet, that the child is related to society rather than to God and is made aware of social evils rather than personal sin.

Dr. Edward Rogers of England, in one of the highest reaches of masterly analysis attained in the World Methodist Conference of 1956, declared that political and economic systems are molded by what humans want — be it God or gold! In other words, persons make the institution rather than the reverse; and although just institutions facilitate personal righteousness, they cannot guarantee that righteousness. William Arthur was right a full century ago when he said that institutions do not make good men, but good men create good institutions.

The neglect of the vertical, that inevitably follows a too exclusive concern for the horizontal in religion, Dr. Rogers puts in these words:

> What went wrong with the "Social Gospel" in the generation immediately past was that it put "social" first and a diluted "gospel" second. Men and women of noble intention strove to implement the Sermon on the Mount while pushing into the background the Cross and the Resurrection: and found that their fine phrases and benevolent exhortations splashed ineffectively on the stubborn rocks of sin.

How about the minority groups in the Methodist movement which have not shifted their primary emphasis from personal to social Christianity? Have they gone to the opposite extreme of indifference to the demands of social religion? Some would have it so, and yet the two principal minority Methodist bodies born in America had their origin on issues that involved, among others, such vital social problems as slavery, secrecy, and free seats. As conservative groups, they may not have followed consistently the progressive pattern of their reforming pioneers, but it is our considered judgment that criticism at this point has been overdone.

The social concern of major Methodism seems to lie principally within its leadership. Note that in *per capita* giving to benevolences, major Methodism falls far below the minority Methodist groups. Using foreign missions as an index (because the latest stewardship reports list this item for all reporting groups), we compute that one minority Methodist body gives ten times and another fifteen times the *per capita* giving of major Methodism. We may safely assume that for items not listed in the reports, such as colleges and charitable institutions, comparisons would likewise favor minority Methodist bodies.

Whatever social indifference may have afflicted these smaller groups in past years, the available evidence points to a present effort to maintain both the personal and the social emphases of their Wesleyan heritage.

And whatever may have been its divergences from strictly Wesleyan principles and practices, major Methodism to this day responds to the social impulse its founder gave to Methodism two centuries ago, and it is first among the larger denominations in social action.

A CONCLUDING WORD

John Wesley was a man of balance, well poised in his position on many issues. In the area of our inquiry, he accepted in principle and applied in practice the scriptural synthesis of "faith working by love" in its upward reach to God and its outward reach to all men. In this, he was far in advance of his age; and Henry Carter says Wesley's "doctrine of stewardship has undiminished relevance for Christians in all generations."

Wesley was not an ascetic esteeming poverty and self-affliction as virtues in themselves. He believed in a life to which every worthy interest was tributary and was therefore in full accord with the repeated "whatsoevers" of Paul's Philippian letter

175

(4:8). We glimpse the range of his sympathies in one of his sermons wherein he pictures the man of God as a man of love, saying of him:

> As a citizen of the world he claims a share in the happiness of all the inhabitants of it. Because he is a man, he is not unconcerned with the welfare of any man; but enjoys whatsoever brings glory to God and promotes peace and good-will among men.
>
> *Standard Sermons,* vol. 1, p. 351

Ernst Troeltsch, in *The Social Teaching of the Christian Churches* (1931), points out that although the early Christian apologetic dealt neither with hopes of improving the social order nor with the healing of social ills, and although the summons of Jesus was not to a program of social reform but to individual preparation for the kingdom of God, the development of a social order out of the Christian message was inevitable.

John Wesley in a remarkable way saw the social bearing of the religion of love and established a healthy relationship of the vertical and the horizontal, of the personal and the social in Christian life and experience.

In a letter written in his advancing eighties, as he faced the setting sun, Wesley wrote:

> It is a blessed thing to have fellow travelers to the New Jerusalem. If you cannot find any, you must make them; for none can travel that way alone.

*The personal note attached
to Marston's copy of this sermon
is included for its intimate insight
into the character of the author
and his devoted wife.*

The Mockery of Minimal Righteousness

But he seemed as one that mocked unto his
sons-in-law.   Genesis 19:14

The subject of this pathetic statement is just and righteous Lot whose belated concern for his family's welfare in sinful Sodom provoked his married children to scorn and derision.

Lot had been left fatherless. After his grandfather died, Uncle Abraham became his guardian. Abraham went forth in answer to God's call, not knowing whither — nephew Lot with him. First into Canaan; then when famine came, into Egypt; then back into Canaan. Prosperity; flocks burden the land; clash of herdsmen. The time has come for Lot to go forth "on his own."

Abraham declares, "Let there be no strife . . . for we be brethren. *Is not the whole land before thee? . . .* If thou wilt take the left hand, then I will go to the right; or if thou depart to the right hand, then I will go to the left" (Genesis 13:8-9).

Abraham had organized "a party for God" — and no doubt expected that whichever Lot's choice might

177

be, Lot would be true to God's party. *But Lot chose, not for the party, but for self!*

Westward, to the left, hills and wilderness. Eastward, to the right, a fertile and populous plain — the plain of the River Jordan.

Lot's wife, who later would look longingly back to Sodom, now looked longingly forward to Sodom. We say the last look was fatal, for she perished: *But this first look was more fatal,* for Sodom now entered her heart!

Long into the night in their tent Lot and his wife talked about Uncle Abe's proposition. The children — for their sake it was time to leave the itinerancy and settle down, establish a home. Further nomadic wanderings would jeopardize their children's education, mating, social opportunities. Wandering around with Uncle Abe had been right when they were younger and had no family — especially inasmuch as they had prospered. *But now it is different.* What if Uncle Abe *had* gone forth, not knowing whither he went, a pilgrim and a sojourner, *they* couldn't be rolling stones forever. Down on the plains they would *belong!*

The choice was made; and until the gray of dawn, Lot and his wife laid their plans for the new world they would enter — building air castles over Sodom!

In the morning, Lot reported his choice to Abraham. They settled accounts, divided their affairs, dissolved partnership. Lot and wife and family and herdsmen and flocks and all their baggage headed for the plain. Abraham set his rugged, sun-tanned, and wind-bitten face to the hill-country.

To every man there openeth
A Way, and Ways, and a Way,
And the High Soul climbs the High Way,
And the Low Soul gropes the Low;
And in between, on the misty flats,
The rest drift to and fro.
But to every man there openeth
A High Way and a Low,
And every man decideth
The way his soul shall go.

                          John Oxenham

Lot pitched his tent toward Sodom. He did not at once enter Sodom, but Sodom had already moved into his heart. And so, very soon, he is established there with his family.

Sodom did have its advantages all right. Schools, prosperity, social life. But it was a wicked city, and its corruption vexed the soul of righteous Lot! No place in Sodom for an altar. Abraham had built altars in the wilderness, but of course it is quite different in the city — *some things you just don't do in the city!*

But Lot didn't surrender his standards — *he was a just man.* Inwardly he would hold to his rugged principles *but not make a big fuss about them.* He'd get by all right, even in Sodom!

No altar, no family religion — a just man, was Father Lot, but not ardent in his religion and his worship. Lot was in Sodom to make money — and while making it, he would not give up his religious faith even if he *said* little about his religion. *But* what impressed the growing minds of his children was the money Dad sought and the money Dad got — not Dad's religion!

The children knew in a vague sort of way that Dad was different — that he had some queer ideas of a Supreme Being and of right living that no one else in Sodom shared, and which Mother said he got from an old and rather peculiar uncle he had lived with for many years.

And Mother Lot was engrossed with the social life of Sodom — Oh, no! Of course not the life of the fast set, but of the better and fashionable group. And she was surprised and flattered that these matronly ladies of Sodom, sleek and well groomed, so readily accepted her into their circle. Sometimes she wondered if it was because of Lot's vast herds and the city property he was now acquiring so rapidly — but she quickly put away such thoughts as ungenerous. True, they were amused at some of her scruples — but they were gracious and tolerant, and soon she came to wonder if after all she had not been a little narrow along some lines, such as fashionable dress and just a social game of bridge. Perhaps she had lost her perspective during those years she had been "out in the sticks" following the cramped style of Uncle Abe and Aunt Sarah!

And it really was remarkable how they were getting on in Sodom!

And then, suddenly, there came disaster!

Sodom was pillaged, and Lot and his wife and daughters were carried off northward.

A fugitive carried the word of the plunder of Sodom and the capture of Lot's household to Abraham; who at once organized his servants and herdsmen — 318 in number. And with the swiftness and cunning of a nomad chieftain, for such he was, overtook and routed the army of Chedorlaomer, king of Elam, recaptured Lot, his womenfolk, and his goods.

Lot should have learned his lesson! But Sodom was in his heart and he returned, hoping to recover his lost fortunes. He redoubled his business diligence. He made good in a big way — and perhaps impressed the citizenry of Sodom by having an uncle such as Abraham. Anyway, *they made him judge -mayor!*

This brought the girls (we know nothing of sons) into better and better circles, and one by one they married — men of Sodom, of course.

Lot was still a *righteous man.* He paid one hundred cents on the dollar — and demanded the same from others. He was still vexed with the exceeding sinfulness of the city, *but he was in no position to turn reformer!* He hadn't been elected mayor on a reform ticket — why, no one could be elected on such a ticket in Sodom! If the people of Sodom wanted things the way they were, what could he do but judge their affairs according to their own principles and quietly go about his own business in an upright manner? *When in Rome, do as the Romans do!*

D. L. Moody says of Lot, "He is a representative man. Where you can find one Abraham, one Daniel, one Joshua, you can find a thousand Lots."

Yes, Lot is representative of a type, a shrewd businessman — progressive, somewhat grasping perhaps; but *not corrupt,* even if not generous. Indeed, a *just man.*

— No warmth of enthusiasm.

— No recklessness of faith.

— His feet are on the ground.

He pays his honest debts and thinks he'll get by, both in this life and the next. He's a legalist — a just man — and salvation is his due! We can hear Lot pray — of course not publicly in Sodom˙ — as later did the Pharisee in Jerusalem:

"I thank Thee that I am not as other men about
me here in Sodom;

"I pay my debts; I regard my marriage vows;

"I even pay tithes to Melchizedec."

But Lot's coldly calculating, legalistic compounding of his own righteousness for eternal salvation didn't win his daughters and their husbands. His children were fully sold on Sodom, socially and financially. Soul and body, they *belonged to Sodom!*

Mother Lot was graying somewhat now, and at times had an uneasy feeling that all was not well as she observed her daughters and their gentlemen friends (who one by one became her sons-in-law) completely abandoned to the ways of the younger social set in Sodom.

— Not a thought about God.

— Not a care about eternity.

Eat, drink, and be merry, for tomorrow we die.

And faster throbs the music. More agitated becomes the dance — the dance of death!

> To say of shame — What is it?
> Of virtue — We can miss it!
> Of sin — We can but kiss it
> And it's no longer sin.

* * *

One evening, Mayor Lot was closing his day as judge at the city's gate when strangers arrived. True to the example set for him in olden days by Uncle. Abraham, Lot invited the strangers to his home for the night. (Was there something about these strangers that reminded Lot of the guests Abraham used to entertain?) After some insistence, the strangers turned in to lodge with Lot.

During the night, the lewd men of Sodom attempted to take captive these strange guests of Lot; and from his own doorstep Lot pleaded with them but *to no avail!* He had lost all influence with his wicked townsmen, who railed against him. "This one fellow came in to sojourn, and he will needs be a judge: now will we deal worse with [you than by your guests]" (Genesis 19:9).

What a night of horror it was! Mayor Lot was rescued from his own townsmen, only by the intervention of the angels he was entertaining unawares. And these heavenly messengers, now knowing full well that even "Ten Righteous" could not be mustered in Sodom, announced to Lot the city's doom and urged him to warn his daughters and their husbands to leave the place.

Out into the night Lot made his way to his daughters' houses. Reaching the first, he knocked loudly to arouse the household from deep slumber. Finally a head appeared at the window upstairs, and a voice called, "Who's there? What's wanted?" "It's Father Lot — *Sodom is doomed!* Flee for your lives. Mother and the girls are leaving with me at daybreak. Hurry and join us!"

"But he seemed as one that mocked!"

*   *   *

"Oh, run along home and go to bed where you belong. This night air isn't good for you," I seem to hear the son-in-law mutter to Lot's daughter. And as he turns again to slumber *(this time to sleep the sleep of death)*, "The old man's religion is breaking out on him, poor fool! He's in his dotage."

And to the second daughter's home — and to the third, where he received the same or similar response.

Abraham prevailed for Sodom's salvation, should there be found therein *ten* righteous. Abraham hoped that Lot's just life would have won fifty. *But he assumed, of course, that Lot would have held his own in Sodom* — three daughters and their husbands, the two unmarried girls, Lot and his wife — *ten!*

How long had Lot been in Sodom? Twenty-five to thirty years — *And not a single convert!* A *just man* — living a whole *generation* in one community *and not even holding his own household!*

How long could you live in Sodom without anyone finding God because *you had lived there?*

How long? The answer depends in part upon whether you have any business living in Sodom. If you are in Sodom and God doesn't want you there, *you'll be like Lot!* Perhaps you'll save your own soul *but lose your own household.* You *may* lose your own soul!

But if God calls you into Sodom, He can keep you there — keep your family there — and through you, win others!

*   *   *

Can you picture Lot making his way homeward after repeated mockings by his own children? Dejected, disheartened, despairing. He had prospered in Sodom, but leanness had come to his soul.... That choice long years ago — by it he had saved his own life — *now he is to lose it!* There is no congratulating himself *now* that as a "just" man he has "gotten by" in Sodom.... No rejoicing over his sleek and fertile herds, nor his lucrative and honorable office, nor his progressive business methods by which he has proved that honesty is the best policy.

How well he realizes in this hour that "He that loveth silver shall not be satisfied with silver; nor he that loveth abundance with increase" (Ecclesiastes 5:10).

* * *

The break of day found Lot and wife and daughters stirring about, nervously making preparations to depart from Sodom.... *But how difficult the step that carried them over the threshold of the past* into an uncertain future!... And so they lingered. "But Abraham had stood yet before the Lord" (Genesis 18:22). And the heavenly visitors "laid hold upon his hand, and upon the hand of his wife, and upon the hand of his two daughters; the Lord being merciful unto him: and they brought him forth, and set him without the city. And ... said, Escape for thy life; look not behind thee, neither stay thou in all the plain; escape to the mountain, lest thou be consumed" (Genesis 19:16-17).

*   *   *

But many years before, Lot had faced his choice and chose the plain. Again, he chooses what he thinks is the easy way. He was afraid of the rugged mountains. Years ago, when he was younger, he might have made it in the highlands, for he had been disciplined to the wilderness and hardship. But now he says, "I cannot escape to the mountain, lest some evil take me . . . behold now, this city is near to flee unto, and it is a little one [not a big one like Sodom — not so wicked as Sodom]: O, let me escape thither" (Genesis 19:19-20). His prayer was granted!

*   *   *

"But his wife looked back from behind him, and she became a pillar of salt." Yes, Lot's wife looked back to Sodom, because the Sodom that crept into her heart thirty years ago, when she looked forward to Sodom, *was still in her heart.*

*   *   *

I have been in Pompeii, city of sin where excavators have uncovered two corpses which tell tales of high drama. One, a Roman sentinel, who died at his post. The other a Roman lady, feet turned to the city's gate, but body turned and stooping as though to grasp — what? — her helpless child? No! An aged, faltering parent? No! — *A bag of pearls!* And for that one moment to save her trifles, *Lost! Lost!*

186

Don't sneer at a Bible which records that Lot's wife was turned to a pillar of salt by her delay to look back upon wicked Sodom in flames, when Pompeii, this ancient city of destruction, has yielded to the archaeologist's pick so many corpses frozen into statues by sudden catastrophe.

*　　*　　*

And Lot's wife, staying a moment to look back, is seized by some swift and unknown doom — is frozen, encrusted — in the posture most expressive of her heart's deepest longing!

Would you willingly permit your mortal remains to petrify as a statue expressive of your secret longings, your soul's passion? Thus it was with Lot's wife!

*　　*　　*

Oh, the mockery of minimal righteousness! How many there are like Lot! Just men, *upright* if not *generous; righteous* if not *spiritual-minded.* They are after material success — and frankly admit it — but self-righteously add that they would succeed only within the law. They are neither very good nor very bad. They are *correct, upright, just.* They do not descend to the level of the sinful plain of Sodom — *but too often, their influence fails to check the descent to that level of those they have brought to Sodom with them.* Their place in Sodom is *business,* not a *mission!* And whereas, one man with a passion to save Sodom could succeed in such a mission, another such as Lot — a rigidly just man — *can live in Sodom a generation* and, at its close, *see Sodom wrapped in the flames of hell!* Too many are concerned with *minimal righteousness:* they scheme to get by with just enough religion to get to heaven — *the tragedy!*

> *Couldst thou in vision see*
> *Thyself the man God meant,*
> *Thou never more wouldst be*
> *The man thou art, content.*

The following notation was found attached to Bishop Marston's manuscript of "The Mockery of Minimal Righteousness."

First preached [this message] December 13, 1939, at a District Quarterly Meeting in Greenville, Illinois. When about to begin, the "Mrs. Lot" of Greenville was ushered in and seated in front center — a fashionable and rich woman of the community who was quite taken with my psychology teaching and my speaking. How she enthused over the message! . . . How had I failed?

* * *

My wife was not present that morning, and I ventured the following: "Several years ago I went to live in 'Sodom.' My friends thought I had made Lot's choice. I knew, as definitely as I ever knew God's will at any point in my life, that Sodom was God's choice for me at that time. I would not long dwell upon such a personal item — but I do wish now, when she is not present to check me with one of those wireless signals that some preachers understand, to pay tribute to my wife.

"When I turned toward Sodom in answer to the call of duty — and by Sodom I mean a lucrative position, pleasant living surroundings, and at least for my wife an 'easy time' — she feared that it was not the call of duty and that I would be lost to the church and perhaps to God. I was compelled to go against her tears and entreaties. Of course, then, I went carefully and prayerfully.

"But more! After some time in Sodom, the call came to the 'hill-country,' to hardship, to sacrifice — and Sodom had not gained a foothold in her heart! Even in Sodom, a pilgrim and a stranger! And when that call came — to the service of God and the church — there was nothing else for me but to take my marching orders and march! I say this humbly: Many a man has been lost to the church and has squandered his life, if not lost his soul, because his wife's heart was wed to Sodom!"

Editor's note: Bishop Marston's "Sodom" was Washington, D.C., working for the National Research Council in Child Developement, on a Rockefeller budget. His "hill country" was his call to return to Greenville College as president .

Preached Sunday morning, 1960, Centenary General Conference.
He offered an alternative:
"The Fellowship of True Believers."

The Church As the Body of Christ

> For as we have many members in one body, and all
> members have not the same office: so we, being many,
> are one body in Christ, and every one members one of
> another.   Romans 12:4-5

We speak of the church, not as a consecrated
building, nor a particular place, nor primarily as an
organized body of people, but rather as the fellowship
of true believers in Jesus Christ — His loyal
followers wherever they meet, which sometimes is in
strange places.

I have preached in a rustic log church in the
Superior region of North Michigan, in a structure so
small that thirty-five worshipers are cramped in its
crowded pews. But God meets His people in this
simple wilderness sanctuary.

I have preached in the rough mountain region of
the mid-south at an outpost reached on horseback,
following a flowing creek-bed as the trail to the
mountain's summit. I preached in overalls that
afternoon, which I had worn to protect my more
formal clothes on the journey. But upon arrival at
the preaching place, I knew not how to shed the

overalls without seeming overly particular to those simple but sensitive mountaineers wearing home-spun.

Many years ago I preached in the swamps of the deep south, a place so isolated that the congregation did not know that familiar hymn, "How Firm a Foundation." They did not know the hymn, but they knew the Firm Foundation!

One Sunday afternoon I preached in a mission of Chicago's skid row. An unclean gutter bum came to an altar of prayer and promised God he would put on clean clothes. And he did! Someone directed him to the church where I was to preach that night. He came, dressed as a respectable citizen, and testified to the power of God's grace.

I once preached in an underprivileged village on the shore of the Bay of Naples to an eager congregation of Italian peasants who had long lived in the gloom and superstition of Romanism. Seldom have I met keener interest in the gospel message.

In England's lovely Salisbury Cathedral my heart was warmed in Methodist fashion on a Sunday evening as I sat in a side chapel under the ministry of a member of the Cathedral staff.

In sinful Paris, in the Salvation Army's "City of Refuge" I listened to radiant testimonies and a gospel sermon, the spiritual warmth of which reached me through words of a language I did not understand — but I knew God was there.

We onetime journeyed to an isolated Indian village far from the beaten paths, traveling part of the distance of our journey up a riverbed where the deep sand trapped and stalled our automobile — both going and coming! That night in the village I looked into the dusky faces of a throng of Christians and their heathen neighbors. They were seated on rugs and mats in the main village street, or standing around the fringe — all under a large awning stretched from side to side of Main Street. The Christians worshiped God, praising Him with songs and instruments — both strange to us — but God heard their song, understood their music, and accepted their offering of praise!

I am reminded of a Palm Sunday experience. It was midnight or later when we reached Umri and the hospital compound, after picking our way through the darkness and now and then missing the track. But Sunday morning — Palm Sunday, it was — came with a glorious light. I think I may never again see such a beautiful sight: a throng of villagers and residents of the compound and hospital staff, adults and children, in their colorful oriental robes, singing and waving palm branches in a triumphal march around the spacious compound. And most moving of all, the ceremony concluded with a lovely exercise of song and palms by little children before the Dr. Paul Yardy residence where we were staying. Our souls were blessed, our spirits were refreshed — and God looked down in love upon His children of far-off India who, with children of long ago, would honor His Son!

Where two or three — or two or three hundred or thousand — have met anywhere in the name of Christ, whether in some leafy wilderness tabernacle, some mission hall, or well-appointed church, Christ also is there, sensibly real to the fellowship of

Christians who are His continuing body here on earth. But how is this possible? We turn for the answer to the first Christian fellowship, to the origin of the Christian church.

Recall the disciples' dismay and discouragement which reached black despair, when Jesus was treacherously betrayed, shamefully arrested and tried, unjustly sentenced, and brutally hanged.

The disciples had thought that Jesus was soon to overthrow the power of Rome and establish an earthly kingdom — but their hopes now lay in ashes at their feet.

Then came the Resurrection and their Lord's repeated appearances, stirring within them again the hope that, after all, He would establish His throne in Jerusalem. Then one day several weeks after the Resurrection, He led the Eleven from their upper room lodging in Jerusalem — out of the city and to the Mount of Olives. Imagine their eager expectancy as they followed Jesus over this familiar trail and up the slope of this beloved Mount. They must have sensed an impending event of vast importance. Is everything now to be set right? At last — at long last — will Jesus put His enemies to rout and establish His earthly rule?

And when they were assembled on the Mount, with animation they asked, "Lord, will you do it now? Will you now restore the kingdom to Israel?" Their pleading was urgent, insistent, much as a child begs a parent, "Dad, Mom, do it now! Please!"

But in very plain terms Jesus told them that times and seasons were entirely in God's hand, but there was something for them to do. They had asked

Him now to set up His kingdom, and He had turned the task to them with these words: "Ye shall be witnesses unto me both in Jerusalem, and in all Judea, and in Samaria, and unto the uttermost part of the earth" (Acts 1:8).

His work on earth has now become theirs. What they had asked Him to do, He commissions them to do. How often we plead, "Lord, wilt Thou. . . ?" And we call our clamor "prayer," but it prevents our hearing Him say, "But ye. . . !"

Jesus in effect has told His disciples that they are to continue His life on earth. But not one of them stepped forth to volunteer, "Lord, here am I, send me!"

How could they do His work on earth? Only by having the power that was His — the power of His Spirit — the Holy Spirit. The Scriptures make clear that this was His power; that at the baptism the Spirit descended like a dove upon Him; that after His baptism, He was led of the Spirit into the wilderness; that after the wilderness temptation, He returned in the power of the Spirit into Galilee; that in Nazareth, when He was handed the Book for synagogue worship, He found the place where it is written, "The Spirit of the Lord is upon me"; and that He made specific application of these words to himself and His ministry.

And now, on Olivet, He has promised the Eleven the same power of the Spirit by which He had wrought and taught, that they might carry on His task when He had gone. He said to them, "But ye shall receive power, after that the Holy Ghost is come. . ." (Acts 1:8).

And ten days later was Pentecost, and the promise was fulfilled in the outpouring of the Holy Ghost upon them all. This was the birthday of the Church. Later, Paul was to write: "For by one Spirit are we all baptized into one body" (I Corinthians 12:13).

This body was not a lifeless corpse but a living organism with the Holy Spirit its animating life-principle. Only through the Church as His body could Christ's ministry on earth continue. As the poet has written in familiar lines:

> He has no hands but our hands
> To do His work today;
> He has no feet but our feet
> To lead men in His way;
> He has no tongue but our tongues
> To tell men why He died;
> He has no help but our help
> To bring them to His side.

To make clear the nature and purpose of the Church as Christ's continuing earthly body, we note *three pairs of contrasting opposites* that are necessary to the Church's health and its effective functioning.

UNITY IN DIVERSITY

In this body of Christ there is *unity in diversity*. At Pentecost, when drawn together by the Spirit's baptism to form the body of Christ, the disciples and the rest of the one hundred twenty were not pressed into a mold to make them identical units like bricks in a wall. (There is no work of grace that operates as a steamroller to flatten out all wrinkles of individuality and personality.) But each person

195

retained his peculiar constitutional traits and special gifts, now cleansed of self and augmented by the power of the Holy Spirit.

Yes, this body of Christ has many members or organs, each with a distinctive office. Paul wrote to the Corinthian church concerning this diversity, setting forth the distinctive functions of hand and foot, eye and ear, and warning of painful discord if any member should come to regard another member as inferior or unnecessary.

Some in the Corinthian church were much exercised about their strange and spectacular gifts, which led them to self-display and arrogance but contributed nothing to the growth or health of the body. Paul pointedly wrote to them, "... forasmuch as ye are zealous of spiritual gifts, seek that ye may excel to the edifying of the church" (I Corinthians 14:12). Here is the corrective to unbridled enthusiasm and disruptive fanaticism: Let those who are zealous to exercise superior gifts, subordinate the same to the building up of the body rather than asserting them for self-glory, to the disruption of the unity of the Spirit in the Church.*

To the Ephesian church Paul portrayed the unity in diversity of the body of Christ. There is one Lord, one faith, one baptism, one body, one Spirit, one God and Father of all. But, there are differing gifts by which some are made apostles, some prophets, some evangelists, some pastors and teachers; for the perfecting of the saints, for the work of humble service, for the building up of the body of Christ

*This paragraph was not a part of the sermon but was in the accompanying notes. — E. M.

until all come to unity of faith in knowing the Son of God, to mature manhood — even the measure of the stature of full grown men in Christ. (See Ephesians 4:4-15.)

Here in Ephesians Paul also describes the unity of many organs and parts as the whole body firmly knit together by that which every joint supplies, each part working properly with others, as the entire body builds itself up in love.

How perfect is this picture of a healthy, harmonious, fully articulated, Spirit-filled, and growing church! There are no detached fragments, no members out-of-joint, no amputated organs — and none attached to the body as mere appendages, serving no function. Each is fully integrated with the body. It belongs!

With any member absent or out-of-joint, Christ's body, the Church, is incomplete and hampered in its functioning. In measure, it is lame, halt, blind! Every one of us has his function in the fellowship of the Church, a function none other can serve as God intended you and me to serve.

The Day of Pentecost in the year A.D. 30 was the birthday of the Church. But only as Pentecost comes personally to individual members of the Church today will the Church endure and succeed as the body of Christ. Let us not blame spiritual decline on the Church as some vague abstraction, hovering in the mists over our heads. Pentecost is an urgently personal matter. You and I are the Church! Spiritual decline in the Church means that you and I, the members of the Church, have declined spiritually!

In this fellowship, the body of Christ, is found

another synthesis of opposites, the synthesis of *love* and *discipline*.

LOVE AND DISCIPLINE

Love makes the Church an inclusive fellowship. Its arms extend outward, even as the arms of the Cross — ever open to the whole wide world, and never closing to encircle some select class or race or color. To the Galatians whose religion was a closed circle, Paul wrote:

> For ye are all the children of God by faith in Christ Jesus. For as many of you as have been baptized into Christ [Phillips: have put on the family likeness of Christ]. There is neither Jew nor Greek, there is neither bond nor free, there is neither male nor female: for ye are all one in Christ. (3:26-28)

A lawyer once sought to fix love's limit by asking Jesus, Who is my neighbor? Jesus made it clear by His account of the Good Samaritan that love does not seek limits, but outlets; love seeks not hedges and line-fences to bound neighborliness, but an open range with no limiting barrier.

Because of love's dynamic outreach, the body of Christ is normally a growing body, not static and stunted. And yet, so often we expect little increase, or we seek to satisfy ourselves with merely "holding our own." A striking but unfortunate slogan held favor among us for years: "a clean rather than a big work" — as if there could not be both! Far too many imbibed the slogan's suggestion that the church cannot be a growing body and at the same time be kept clean.

198

But how was it with the early Church? In response to the first sermon preached in the Holy Spirit dispensation, there were three thousand converts! If some had been there whom you and I know, they would have said, "Brother Peter must have compromised the truth today, for three thousand would never take the way in one service. This work cannot be genuine — these converts will never stand!" But what does the record say? We read,

> And they continued steadfastly in the apostles' doctrine and fellowship, and in breaking of bread, and in prayers. Acts 2:42

Well, these converts measured up to some very high standards: apostolic doctrine; fellowship with the saints; continuing prayer. May the Lord deliver us from the idea that the Church cannot maintain discipline and yet grow! If this were true, Christianity from its beginning was doomed to decline and to early extinction.

Now let us notice the place of *discipline*. Without discipline, the body loads itself with fat, becomes flabby and slothful. The discipline of truth is necessary — truth in both doctrine and conduct, in both Christian belief and in Christian living. Without the restraints of discipline, love becomes soft and indulgent, excusing error in doctrine and worldliness in life; even as discipline on the other hand, without the compassion of love, is harsh and impersonal. Paul expressed the proper synthesis of love and discipline in the phrase, "speaking the truth in love." The Church must declare the truth in the areas both of doctrine and life, but it must declare that truth in love.

Evangelicals in general hold to the discipline of doctrine, and they recognize the duty of the organized Church to require a confession of faith, a testimony of belief. But not all Evangelicals conceive that it is equally the responsibility of the Church to define, as conditions of church membership and as a witness to the world, how a Christian should live. But it is clear that the New Testament Church maintained its discipline in both areas. Belief and life may not be separated without danger to the health of the body of Christ.

Young churches in general have been a struggling, pioneering, and persecuted minority, growing strong through the discipline of adversity, loving intensely and ready to die for the truth. But with strength and prosperity in older areas of the Church, too often there has come a settling down to ordinary living and ordinary devotion.

In his day John Wesley foresaw clearly that the simplicity and frugality of devoted Christian living would bring material prosperity, the effect of which on Methodism gave him great concern. When eighty-seven years of age, he wrote this solemn warning that may well be pondered by us today:

> The Methodists grow more and more self-indulgent, because they grow rich. . . . And it is an observation that admits of few exceptions, that nine in ten of these (who become rich) decreased in grace, in the same proportion as they increased in wealth.

200

INWARD RENEWAL
AND OUTWARD EXPRESSION

And now we come to our third union of opposites. The body of Christ must be maintained in health by *inward renewal* and *outward expression,* that is, by worship and service, by getting and giving. We have just noted that persecution and hardship are a healthy discipline but that prosperity and success bring danger of spiritual decline. When outer enemies no longer threaten the Church's very existence, and thus keep it alert and active, there is danger that ease and indulgence will bring on a creeping, degenerative softening of moral and spiritual fiber. Emerson once declared that the health of a man is an equality of inlet and outlet, a balance of gathering and giving; but hoarding means tumor and disease.

Is it inevitable that the body of Christ should decline in health with growth in numbers and increase in material prosperity? The Laodicean church, which John wrote about in Revelation 3, was far too typical. It boasted, "I am rich, and increased with goods, and have need of nothing" (v. 17a). But the Spirit said, thou "knowest not that thou art wretched, and miserable, and poor, and blind, and naked" (v. 17b). Material prosperity had brought on spiritual bankruptcy — and Laodicea didn't know it! But such bankruptcy is not inevitable, thank God! For the Lord said to this very church, "I counsel thee to buy of me gold tried in the fire, that thou mayest be rich; and white raiment, that thou mayest be clothed" (v. 18).

Concerning the almost inevitable decline of

spirituality with increase in material prosperity, Wesley asked, "But is there no way to prevent this? ... I can see only one possible way. ... Do you gain all you can, and save all you can? Then you must in the nature of things grow rich. Then if you have any desire to escape the damnation of hell, *give all you can*."

This means stewardship of our earning powers and of our earnings. How prone are we to say that the gold in the hills belongs to our God, and the cattle on the hills also. And this is true — these are His by His right of creatorship and by His continuing sovereignty over His creation. But in building His church here on earth, God has no gold but yours and mine — no cattle but what we hold in title, not of ownership but of stewardship. This is what stewardship means — that we are workers together with God! Great is this mystery of godliness, that God should make the success of His program on earth depend upon our cooperation. This thought is expressed in the following lines:

> God builds no churches! By His plan
> That labor has been left to man.
>
> . . . .
>
> The humblest church demands its price
> In human toil and sacrifice.
>
> . . . .
>
> The humblest spire in mortal ken,
> Where God abides, was built by men.
> And if the church is still to grow,
> Is still the light of hope to throw
> Across the valleys of despair,

Men still must build God's house of prayer.
God sends no churches from the skies,
Out of our hearts must they arise!

Edgar A. Guest

The safeguard against spiritual decline when wealth and talent and social influence increase in the church is this: Let every member of the body of Christ commit his every possession — time, talents, as well as gold — to the service of God, to the edification of the body of Christ. This is entire consecration!

But this is not enough! The consecration of every power and possession to the service of Christ and His Church, however full the consecration and however strenuous the service, will be ineffectual unless, deep within, we have inexhaustible resources of the Spirit. Our spiritual life must move deeper than our fullest service. The inner life must constantly be renewed by prayer and worship if our service is to be more than rank foliage and colorful bloom — if it is to bear rich fruitage.

This worship we so much need, if we are to have strength for effective service, must be more than occasional breaks in our strenuous American activism by which to induce relaxation through religious symbolism, majestic music, and stereotyped ritual. As the Christian fellowship moves from simple, primitive houses of worship to more adequate and sometimes elaborate sanctuaries, history discloses there is a tendency for the sensate and the liturgical to take dominance over the spiritual and the spontaneous.

Some people are like a friend of mine who had wandered far from her early Christian training, and now, in middle life, hoped that she was religious because she was moved by pipe organ music! But there is a natural, instinctive religious awe in experiencing the majestic and beautiful in nature and in art. This is common to all mankind, apart from grace, and those who seek therein their basis of Christian assurance are deceiving themselves with the Laodiceans to believe that they need nothing when in fact they are void of the Spirit.

May our churches never substitute the stone of natural, sensate worship for the bread of personal communion with God!

In these words, an unknown poet has well expressed the synthesis of spiritual worship and fruitful service:

> Come ye yourselves apart and rest awhile,
>   Weary, I know it, of the press and throng;
> Wipe from your brow the sweat and dust of toil,
>   And in My quiet strength again be strong.
>
> Come ye and rest; the journey is too great,
>   And ye will faint beside the way and sink;
> The bread of life is here for you to eat,
>   And here for you the wine of love to drink.
>
> Then fresh from concourse with your Lord return,
>   And work till daylight softens into even;
> The brief hours are not lost in which ye learn
>   More of your Master and His rest in heaven.

Following is a review of the course we have pursued:

1. The true Church of our living Lord is not

limited to material structures nor sacred places, nor is it conditioned by the number of worshipers nor by their stations in life. The Church is where Christ by His Spirit meets with the fellowship of obedient and faithful believers.

2. This fellowship of believers is the continuing body of Christ here on earth; a body of which Christ is the Head, and His Spirit the living principle. And only through this fellowship, as Christ's continuing body, can His ministry on earth continue.

3. There are three pairs of contrasting opposites, the synthesis of which is necessary to the health and growth of this body, the Church:

   a. This body of Christ is a *unity in diversity*. The body has many members with different functions to perform, all contributing to the building up of the body but with painful discord when any member seeks its own glory or welfare rather than the health and increase of the body itself.

   b. The body of Christ brings together in harmonious synthesis the outgoing *love* and the restraint of *discipline* — an inclusive love that is disciplined by truth, and a discipline of truth in both belief and life, tempered by love.

   c. The Church, Christ's body, is a balance or synthesis of worship and service; of getting and giving; of *inward renewal* and *outward expression*. If the outward growth and material prosperity of the church are not to lead to spiritual decline, there must be the consecration of every power and of all possessions to the service of Christ. And moreover, this service must be vitalized and made fruitful by our maintaining a vital experience of God through personal communion with Him.

CONCLUSION

Against this background of cardinal principles underlying the true Church of Christ, we conclude by briefly applying these principles to the Free Methodist Church which is now concluding one century and peering hopefully into its second century.

The Free Methodist Church, while definitely denominational in its clear-cut distinctives, is not sectarian or exclusive in spirit. Its arms are open wide, even as the arms of the Cross. Its basic law (constitution) maintains the inclusiveness of the Christian fellowship by recognizing that Christ the great Shepherd has other sheep than those in the Free Methodist fold.

And the more intimate fellowship within its own enclosure includes those of different nations, races, cultures, and economic classes. This follows properly from the proclamation sounded forth from its *Book of Discipline* nearly a century ago: "To civilized and savage, bond and free, black and white, the ignorant and the learned, is freely offered this great salvation."

The marvelous *unity* of fellowship in the *diversity* of race and color, nation and culture, was remarkably exhibited in the recent Asia Conference where a warm fellowship prevailed among nationals of different countries. The Conference was a corrective to any delusion of national or racial superiority that some might have brought with them. The Christian poise and dignity with which the nationals carried themselves, notwithstanding their different cultures, demonstrated the unity of the body we are now calling World Fellowship of Free Methodist Churches. Foot and hand, eye and ear, all realized their need for one another, and the entire body built itself up in love. We could but conclude that in its many national churches, World Free Methodism has elements of great strength, and that because of what we have already called the growing edge of the church in other nations, God has a purpose and a mission for Free Methodism in its second century.

But Free Methodism means, not alone the inclusiveness of *love,* but also the restraints of *discipline.* These restraints are those standards of doctrine and life which are necessary to the health and growth of the body of Christ. We need not review these in detail, but simply give their central thrust.

1. We hold to the scriptural standard of sound doctrine, defining our faith to include Christian holiness in the Wesleyan tradition. "And the very God of peace sanctify you wholly; and I pray God your whole spirit and soul and body be preserved blameless unto the coming of our Lord Jesus Christ (I Thessalonians 5:23).

2. We hold to the scriptural standard of holy living, witnessing our faith in a disciplined restraint that sharply separates the Christian from the world. "But . . . be ye holy in all manner of conversation" (I Peter 1:15). "And be not conformed to this world" (Romans 12:2).

207

3. We hold to the scriptural standard of Christian experience, possessing our faith as an inner assurance of cleansing and power. "But ye shall be baptized with the Holy Ghost" (Acts 1:5). "And they were all filled with the Holy Ghost" (Acts 2:4).

This inner experience is the central core of *inward renewal*, which expresses itself, and in turn is invigorated by its *outward expression*, in worship. Accordingly:

4. We hold to the scriptural standard of acceptable worship, expressing our faith in the simplicity and freedom of the Spirit. "God is a Spirit: and they that worship him must worship him in spirit and in truth" (John 4:24). "O worship the Lord in the beauty of holiness" (Psalm 96:9).

This inner experience of cleansing and power, if spiritual health is to be maintained and the church is to grow, must be expressed not only in worship but also in service. Therefore:

5. We hold to the scriptural standard of devoted stewardship, demonstrating our faith in full consecration of self and possessions to the service of God and man. "For as the body without the spirit is dead, so faith without works is dead also" (James 2:26). "I will show thee my faith by my works" (James 2:18).

* * *

— Let the Free Methodist Church ever maintain a unity of love in all the diversity of races and classes of mankind, recognizing the important service of each to the welfare of the body, ignoring or scorning none as inferior or unimportant.

— Let the arms of the Church ever extend

outward in love, while it maintains, without compromise, the disciplines of sound doctrine and of holy living.

— Let the Free Methodist Church ever place central in personal experience the assurance of inner cleansing and the Holy Spirit's power, and let it give expression to the same both in acceptable worship to God and in a full consecration for service to God and man.

Then, one day (according to Ephesians 5:26-27), Christ will present us to himself, sanctified and cleansed by the washing of water by the Word, a glorious church, not having spot or wrinkle or any such thing, but holy and without blemish.

Redeeming the Time
in Evil Days

Ephesians 5:15-16

Several years ago, during a convention in Santa Cruz, the convention group one afternoon journeyed to the nearby redwood forest to view some of the world's oldest and largest living forms, the giant redwoods — some of them three hundred feet tall, five thousand years old.

It was a rewarding experience. The convention group scattered in smaller companies to wander at will through the forest. But before leaving, all assembled at a circle of trees united at their base to form a columned "cathedral."

The Light and Life Evangelistic Quartet was with us in the convention, and we listened as the centuries even before Abraham were echoed in the strains of the quartet's stirring number, "More than conquerors are we, Through the blood of Christ our ransom." Then we joined in prayer, the sacred hush of millenniums spreading over us and settling down upon us.

Now and again in the confused foreground of our restless age, when redeeming the time for many means a faster pace to an unknown destination, we need to seek the perspective that comes from considering God's purposes. Not always do they ripen fast — but always, they ripen!

Someone has said that the logic of an eddy has everything on its side except the knowledge of rivers. Caught in the swirling eddies of our own frenzied and futile endeavors, we mistakenly think that we have the compelling answers to the meaning and purpose of life. We need then to break from the eddy's circling grip, to join the mighty, forward-sweeping current of God's unfolding plan.

The theme of our message deals with man's relationship to time, and time's relationship to eternity, and raises the question, How are we to live today, when there may be no tomorrow?

A woman once asked John Wesley, "Mr. Wesley, what would you do if you knew that tomorrow at midnight you would be called hence to meet your God?" His reply we leave to a later point in the message.

But will there be a tomorrow? This ominous question haunts our age — an age of great concern for security. Think of it! In a day when man commands greater power over the forces of nature than ever before in human history, he feels most insecure — he is most afraid!

There are differing answers to our question, How are we to live today, when there may be no tomorrow? Let us note four principal responses, the first three wrong, and then the answer of Paul the Apostle as stated in our text.

1. *There are those who surrender to the clamor of the flesh and live only for today – the now.*

Such have no concern for tomorrow nor for the hereafter. For them, redeeming the time is to "live it up" each moment. Without hope and without God in the world, they take as their motto, "Let us eat, drink, and be merry, for tomorrow we die!"

These persons seek to redeem time by speed. But time in our day is not lost because we are slowing down. Speed mania possesses modern man. He has traveled a long way from the covered wagon, the top-buggy, the automobile, the airplane — and now he is venturing into space!

What happens when we attempt to beat time with speed? We grow old while we are yet young. On his thirty-third birthday, Lord Byron, who had lived in the way of the flesh, wrote in his diary, "I go to bed with a heaviness of heart at having lived so long and to so little purpose."

Life should have four dimensions:
(1) Height, the upward reach of faith
(2) Depth, the foundation of truth and virtue
(3) Breadth, the open arms of love for all mankind
(4) That length of eternity which begins in time

By living only in the *now,* life's dimensions shrink and shrivel to a mere point — the passing moment. This is the narrowly constricted eddy, not the ongoing current of the river which flows on to endless eternity.

Those who seek life only in the *now* are not concerned with holiness and God; they "work all uncleanness with greediness." This is not the way to live today, when there may be no tomorrow.

2. *There are those who ignore the now in a*

212

frenzied concern for holiness and their own salvation.

They are the sensitive souls who yearn for holiness and God, but tend to ignore human need by isolating themselves from the world of human affairs.

The Psalmist David knew the pull of temptation to withdraw from society and seek seclusion. He has told us about it in these words:

> Oh that I had wings like a dove! For then would I fly away, and be at rest. Lo, then would I wander far off, and remain in the wilderness. . . . I would hasten my escape from the windy storm and tempest. . . . For I have seen violence and strife in the city.   Psalm 55:6-9

But sin is not a matter of geography, of place, of where you are, but of what you are at the central core of your being. Many a man (and woman) has sought to escape sin and achieve holiness in the wilderness hut or the monastery cell; but there, in his loneliness, he has come face to face with himself — and failure, if not sin.

In times of moral and social disintegration such as the present period of society, there is the peculiar danger that pious folk will seek for a bomb shelter for protection against a buffeting, tragic world of sin. But withdrawal from the world is no way to live today when there may be no tomorrow!

3. *There are those who despair of the now, awaiting deliverance in some future dispensation.*

These, also, are religious folk, but unlike the retiring pietists just mentioned, they understand that the Christian must live in the *now;* they accept the present order as inevitable, maintaining that even the Christian must share this world's corruption, having no hope of religious revival or social reform in this dispensation.

But it is not God's purpose that any should perish; and although the collapse of civilization threatens, God has not ordained it. If it comes, it will be the result of man's rebellion against God and righteousness.

When, in the desperation of our pessimism, we rely upon the collapse of decency and social order to hasten Christ's return to establish a new order, we thwart the divine purpose by laying down the burden of righteousness which He has committed to us to bear.

How then are we to redeem the time when there may be no tomorrow

—if not by "living it up" in the *now?*

—if not by turning our backs on the *now?*

—if not by despairing of the *now?*

4. *We are to redeem the time by buying it up for Eternity!*

Redeeming the time is living in the *now* with eternal values in view. The *now* has meaning for the *forever!* This life has meaning because of Eternity. Those who say that the Christian way is too otherworldly are mistaken; for apart from the spiritual and the Eternal, life is utterly meaningless.

Let man think of this life as mere physiology; let him view the drama of human history as "a brief and transitory episode in the life of the meanest of the planets"; let him view man as "an ape that chatters to himself glibly of kinship with archangels while filthily he digs for groundnuts"; and let him

214

view the human race as "a bit of the organic scum of one small planet" — and mankind swiftly sinks into the muck and mire of the jungle.

But let man see himself as the handiwork of God with a high and holy eternal destiny, and he may come, in the phrasing of the Apostle Paul, "unto the measure of the stature of the fulness of Christ."

Think of it! The Christian is to strive right here in *time* toward the goal of *eternity!* And the work he begins in *time,* if he builds with gold and silver and precious stones, will endure and be consumated in *eternity!* More than a dressing room for *eternity, time* is the very laboratory of the eternal.

And now we give you John Wesley's answer to the woman who asked him how he would spend his remaining time on earth, if he knew he were to die at midnight tomorrow:

> How, madam? Why, just as I intend to spend it now. I should preach this night at Gloucester, and again at five tomorrow morning. After that I should go to Tewksbury, preach in the afternoon, and meet with the societies in the evening. I should then repair to friend Martin's house who expects to entertain me, converse with the family as usual, retire to my room at ten o'clock, commend myself to my heavenly father, lie down to rest, and wake up in glory.

* * *

We are called, not merely to save our own souls, but to invest our talents, our energies, all our resources, to building our eternity. Too often our concern is only to be saved ourselves, and then we settle down into a comfortable and ordinary way of

Christianity. We do not build for eternity but for the *now*, hoping for a passage to heaven someday. We do not deposit our treasure there as an eternal investment — preferring to consume it here on our desires.

*   *   *

What is the meaning of this message for you?
1. *You are not to surrender to the world – to the spirit of the age – to the now!*
2. You are not to be indifferent to the world and its need, in smug enjoyment of your own saintliness.
3. You are not to despair of the world, surrendering to its corruption while claiming Christ's imputed righteousness while awaiting His return.
4. But you *are* to wage a vigorous assault on the sin and corruption of the *now,* offering in dedication to God a free, untrammeled channel for the passage of God's Spirit on the world in revival and renewal.

This is meeting the challenge of both the now and the eternal.